Technology Hacks for Fitness, Sports and Outdoor Activities:

Innovative Projects from PhysTech 2024

Shun Nagata and Sarasa Ouchi (Editors)

Binnovative Innovation Book Series

Cover Design: Rimi Yoshikawa

ISBN: 979-8-3031-7444-3

Table of Contents

Foreword

PhysTech is the second student-organized public hackathon that Binnovative has sponsored, following the success of AnimalHack 2023. As Binnovative's CEO, I am thrilled to see young, enthusiastic students not only plan and execute these events but also showcase their innovative ideas to an even broader audience through the publication of this second book.

The PhysTech hackathon presentations, held on June 30, left me genuinely amazed by the participants' pitches. Their ability to identify unique problems and craft solutions using technology was truly impressive.

As I often emphasize, design thinking is crucial in product development, especially for those creating new products or solutions. Understanding the real problem—knowing who your customer is and what challenges they face—is essential.

In today's world, learning technology—whether it be IoT, programming, or other areas—has become a standard part of education. However, learning can sometimes feel monotonous for kids. By setting a theme like Physical Activity and Technology and encouraging them to create their own solutions, we not only hone their technical skills but also strengthen their problem-solving abilities.

Looking ahead, I hope Binnovative can continue providing opportunities for young enthusiasts to shape the future. I want to express my deep gratitude to everyone who supported this event, including our judges. I eagerly anticipate another inspiring PhysTech presentation next year.

Eriko Nishimoto
Founder and CEO of Binnovative

Preface

This book showcases a selection of award-winning projects from PhysTech 2024. PhysTech is a student-organized online hackathon for anyone who does, watches, analyzes, and promotes any physical activities – including sports, workouts, fitness exercises, casual hobbies/pastimes, and recreational adventures. We decided to create our own hackathon since we were frustrated by the scarcity of international, open hackathons dedicated to physical activities.

The inaugural edition of PhysTech took place online on June 30, 2024. For its launch, we formed a team of the following six organizers from the New York and Boston areas in March 2024.

- Hiroki Kudara
- Shun Nagata (co-chair)
- Rei Nagata
- Koki Okusha
- Sarasa Ouchi (co-chair)
- Hanna Suzuki
- Nikichi Tsuchida

We started by organizing an online meeting to decide on a name for the hackathon. Each of us brought ideas for a name that would fit the hackathon's theme, and we came up with the name we have now after careful consideration. Once the name of the hackathon was chosen, we divided up the roles, created a logo for the hackathon, built a DevPost page to make announcements, set up a Discord channel to communicate with participants, produced merchandise using the logo, prepared an online form for hackathon registration, formed a panel of judges, and made certificates for project presenters. We spent about three months preparing for the event.

PhysTech 2024 attracted 201 participants at DevPost.com and received 23 project submissions from the US, Singapore, Pakistan, Japan, India and Vietnam. We invited 11 of them for project presentations. At the hackathon event, nine participants gathered online and gave 10-minute presentations each in front of judges and other hackathon participants. They received the following awards. Congratulations!

- *Grand Prix*:
    - Anshul Kotagiri, "PushUpPro - The best way to work out!"
- *2nd Place*:
    - Nikichi Tsuchida, "Fencing Acceleration Tracker!"
- *3rd Place*:
    - Hanna Suzuki, "Portable WBGT Tracker for Outdoor Athletes in the Heat"
- *Honorable Mention*:
    - Hiroki Kudara, "Soccer Display"
- *Excellence in Research Award*:
    - Shun Nagata, "RCV Visualizer"
- *Excellence in Entrepreneurship Award*:
    - Eshan Aditya Vasipalli, "Active+"
    - Don Tjandra, "TaijiFlow"
- *Excellence in Creativity Award*:
    - Hanna Suzuki, "Glow in the Dark Skateboard"
- *Emerging Talent Award*:
    - Rei Nagata, "Fishing Tracker"

We contacted these prize winners to see if they are interested in publishing book chapters that summarize their projects. This book compiles the chapters from eight of them.

Chapter 1, entitled "Glow in the Dark Skateboard: a Futuristic and Smart Skateboard", is authored by Hanna Suzuki. It represents a smart and futuristic upgrade to the traditional skateboard. By integrating a Raspberry Pi computer, accelerometer, electroluminescent wire, and LED lights, this innovative skateboard senses its orientation and adjusts its lighting patterns accordingly. This design not only adds an entertaining visual element but also enhances safety by increasing visibility at night.

In Chapter 2, Rei Nagata describes "Fishing Tracker," a Raspberry Pi-powered device designed to determine the optimal times for fishing by displaying crucial factors such as tide times, air temperature, and humidity. This system integrates various components to operate efficiently, running Python code to fetch data from online services and display it on a digital message board.

Chapter 3 reports "Fencing Priority Referee: A Wearable Sensor for Data-centric Priority Judgment," which Nikichi Tsuchida worked on for fencing. It is a lightweight and wearable device designed to determine priority in foil fencing when two fencers land simultaneous attacks. This system integrates a Raspberry Pi and an accelerometer to track body movements and detect the moment of attack using a threshold-based algorithm implemented in Python. The device enhances fencing practice by offering clear judgments on priority, eliminating confusion, and improving training efficiency.

In Chapter 4, Shun Nagata describes the "RCV Visualizer," which is a Raspberry Pi powered system with an aimed audience for baseball analysts and anyone who watches baseball. The system implements a new batting performance statistic called Runs Created Value (RCV) and displays RCV values for MLB batters. It helps find players with abilities that cannot be seen in other statistics, predict their performance in the future, and compare them to others and the whole league.

Chapter 5 states "Portable WBGT Tracker for Outdoor Athletes in the Heat" developed by Hanna Suzuki. It is a portable device designed to measure and display the Wet Bulb Globe Temperature (WBGT), indicating heat stress on the human body in direct sunlight. This system integrates a Raspberry Pi running Python code to download WBGT forecasts from the National Oceanic and Atmospheric Administration (NOAA) and display them on an e-paper screen. The device helps outdoor athletes monitor environmental conditions and take necessary precautions to enhance safety with preventing heat-related illnesses during outdoor activities.

In Chapter 6, Vasipalli Eshan Aditya describes "Active+," which is a user-friendly web application designed to promote fitness and help users achieve their fitness goals. By integrating the Fitbit API, Active+ ensures reliable health data display, addressing common issues of poor health management and confusing metrics found in other health-tracking applications. This system features an intuitive design with aesthetically pleasing concentric circles for data visualization, making it accessible and effective for all demographics, and simplifying health tracking for better user engagement and improved fitness outcomes.

Chapter 7 reports "PushUpPro," which Anshul Kotagiri worked on to combine computer vision technology with a user-friendly web interface to enhance fitness training. This system integrates Streamlit for the frontend and utilizes OpenCV and MediaPipe's pose estimation model to accurately detect and analyze body positions during push-ups. By providing real-time feedback on form quality and repetition count, it ensures users can improve their technique and track their progress effectively. With seamless navigation and immediate visual feedback, this tool caters to both fitness enthusiasts and beginners.

In Chapter 8, Hiroki Kudara utilizes a Raspberry Pi and an e-paper display to create a personalized and efficient way to monitor real-time statistics for a specific soccer player. By integrating an API from native-stats.org, the system "Soccer Display" enables users to track their favorite player's recent performances, including match scores, opponents, and game dates. This tool is designed to help soccer enthusiasts stay updated on player stats, offering a practical and customizable solution for keeping up with the sport even when they cannot watch the matches live.

Our special thanks go to our judge, Harish Kamath, for his invaluable comments and suggestions for hackathon participants and his professional judgment on prize winners. We are also grateful for Rimi Yoshikawa, who designed the attractive cover for this book.

We appreciate Binnovative and the PhysTech Advisory Board for helping us organize PhysTech 2024 successfully and complete our hackathon journey with this book. We hope you will find this book informative, enjoyable, and inspiring!

Shun Nagata and Sarasa Ouchi

October 2024

Call for Contributions to PhysTech

`https://binnovative-boston.github.io/phystech/`

PhysTech is a student-organized online hackathon for anyone who does, watches, analyzes and promotes any physical activities – including sports, workouts, fitness exercises, casual hobbies/pastimes and recreational adventures.

PhysTech welcomes any types of physical activities. Sports and physical training are in. Yoga, pilates, ballet? Of course. Swimming, kayaking, cycling, dancing, skateboarding, rock/mountain climbing, hiking, horseback riding? Sure. Fishing, bowling, paddleboarding, scuba diving, rafting, cheer leading, outdoor bird watching, gardening, kite flying, disk golf (frisbee), or cornhole? Why not!

Not only athletes and recreational players/practitioners, but fans, coaches, referees/judges and analysts are also welcome.

PhysTech offers you a platform to address various needs, wants and challenges in physical activities and produce creative solutions (hacks) with technology.

PhysTech welcomes anyone of all ages and all technical skills, from limited experience to advanced. Entry is free.

Expected project topics include, but are not limited to:

- Monitoring and enhancing performance
- Logging and tracking practice, training, and exercise
- Recording, analyzing and communicating activity data
- Applying data analytics to physical activity
- Enhancing fan experience
- Increasing participation/engagement in physical activity
- Promoting health and wellness though physical activity
- Preventing and helping heal from injuries

- Improving dietary and nutritional assistance
- Protecting and improving the environment for physical activity

Solutions can take many different forms such as apps, games, social platforms, web sites/services, devices, sensors, robots, audio/video, data collection/storage, data analysis/forecasts, data visualization, information retrieval, and 3-dimensional modeling/printing.

PhysTech takes place annually – usually in late June. It is hosted by Binnovative, a nonprofit organization in Massachusetts, USA.

Chapter 1

Glow in the Dark Skateboard: A Futuristic and Smart Skateboard

Hanna Suzuki

Bedford High School
Bedford, MA 01730, USA

Abstract

Glow in the Dark Skateboard transforms a traditional skateboard to be futuristic and smart with a small (credit card sized) computer called Raspberry Pi and its peripherals such as an accelerometer, an electroluminescent wire and LED lights. It continuously senses the orientation of the skateboard and changes its lighting pattern according to the current orientation. This chapter describes the features of Glow in the Dark Skateboard and explains how to reproduce it with detailed instructions.

1.1 Introduction

Glow in the Dark Skateboard is a "smart" skateboard that can make skateboarding more fun and safer. It features electroluminescent wire and LED lights that flash brightly. The lights provide an amusing sight of an almost futuristic looking skateboard. It also provides safety precautions. Skateboarding can be dangerous in the dark, especially when there are cars, bikes and pedestrians around. The bright lights can alert other road users of skateboarders when it is hard to see at night.

Glow in the Dark Skateboard changes its lighting pattern in a unique way – based on the skateboard's orientation. When the skateboard is level, LED lights fade in and out between two colors (for example, orange and blue). When the skateboard's orientation is upwards or downwards, it flashes rainbow lights. This is all implemented with Python code that continuously runs on a Raspberry Pi computer to calculate the pitch angle of the skateboard with an accelerometer and flash the LED lights according to the pitch angle.

This chapter guides you to reproduce Glow in the Dark Skateboard by sharing how to assemble hardware components and how to set up software code. Potential future directions and ideas are also given to extend/customize Glow in the Dark Skateboard.

1.2 Hardware Assembly

Glow in the Dark Skateboard is built with a small (credit card sized) computer called Raspberry Pi and its peripheral components. This section explains what components to prepare and how to assemble them.

1.2.1 Required Components

The following components are required to build Glow in the Dark Skateboard.

- Raspberry Pi Zero 2 WH (1x): Purchase a MicroSD card separately to install a Raspberry Pi OS and store data. It does not come with a Raspberry Pi. Amazon Standard Identification Number (ASIN): B09LTDQY2Z. This project uses the "Version 2" of Raspberry Pi Zero (Zero 2 WH), but its Version 1 works too (Zero WH; ASIN: B0CG99MR5W).

- Flirc Aluminum Case for Raspberry Pi Zero (1x): It is highly recommended to place a Raspberry Pi in a case, so it can be firmly attached to the skateboard. ASIN: B08837L144. Adafruit product ID: 4822.

- Portable charger (1x): Any compact and thin charger works. ASIN: B0BYN7357K.

- Micro USB cable (1x): This is to connect the portable charger to Raspberry Pi. A 1-foot (30 cm) cable is recommended. ASIN: B07G934SJ9.

- Pimoroni Blinkt! (1x): This is a bar of 8 LEDs. It fits with Raspberry Pi's 2x20 GPIO header. Adafruit Product ID: 3195. Pimoroni's product Web page: [1].

- Adafruit LIS3DH Accelerometer (1x): This is used to sense the pitch angle of the skateboard. ASIN: B01BU70B64. Adafruit Product ID: 2809.

- JST SH 4-pin 1.0mm-pitch cable (1x): This type of cable is often called Adafruit STEMMA QT or SparkFun Qwiic. They are all compatible. Choose a cable with a JST-SH 4-pin connector on one end and a female socket (for GPIO pins) on the other end. It is used to connect an accelerometer with Raspberry Pi. ASIN: B09PG9MRGX. Adafruit Product ID: 4397.

- GPIO splitter (1x): This is to split Raspberry Pi's GPIO header to two separate headers: one for an LED bar and the other for an accelerometer. ASIN: B0888W3XN4.

- 6-pin right-angle GPIO header (1x): This is convenient to wire an accelerometer and Raspberry Pi. ASIN: B00OE8GTQ8.

- 2"x10" Mounting plate (1x): This is used to mount an accelerometer. Adafruit Product ID: 5780.

- M2.5 screw set (1x): These are used to mount an accelerometer onto a mounting plate. ASIN: B0BL3RW7PJ. Adafruit Product ID: 3299.

- Electroluminescent (EL) wire (1x): A 2.5-meter (8 feet) wire is recommended. Various color choices are available. Adafruit Product ID: 405.

- EL Wire 2xAA inverter (1x): This is to supply power to an EL wire. Adafruit Product ID: 317.

- Velcro strips (4x): These are used to attach a Raspberry Pi, mounting plate, EL wire inverter and portable charger to the skateboard. ASIN: B0010HADEA.

ASINs can be used for product searches at `https://www.amazon.com`, and Adafruit product IDs can be used at `https://www.adafruit.com`.

Fig. 1 shows how Glow in the Dark Skateboard is assembled with the required components.

Raspi

LED
bar

EL wire EL wire Accelerometer Portable
         inverter   charger

Fig. 1: Fully Assembled Glow in the Dark Skateboard

1.2.2 Attaching an Electroluminescent Wire to the Skateboard

First, the EL wire is attached onto the rim of the skateboard with hot glue (Figs. 1 and 2). By attaching it to the rim, it creates the effect that it looks floating like a hoverboard (Fig. 3). However, the wire does not have to be on the rim, it could essentially be put anywhere as long as it does not disrupt the wheels or the top of the deck. The hot glue is secure enough and dries quickly, so a lot does not have to be used. The particular wire and skateboard used had enough to wrap the perimeter of the skateboard, plus a little extra, so the extra is just glued the rest to the middle of the bottom side of the skateboard (Fig. 1).

Fig. 2: EL Wire glued on the Rim of the Skateboard

Fig. 3: EL Wire turned on in the Dark

Note that an EL wire needs to be powered by an AC power source, which a Raspberry Pi does not have. As a result, Glow in the Dark Skateboard uses an inverter (DC-AC converter) that uses two AA batteries to supply AC power for the EL wire. The EL wire is turned on and off manually with a switch on the inverter box, rather than programmatically with Raspberry Pi. The inverter box is attached to the skateboard with a velcro strip (Fig. 1).

1.2.3 Connecting an LED Bar to a Raspberry Pi

Glow in the Dark Skateboard uses Pimoroni Blinkt!, which is a bar of eight LED lights. Each light is individually controllable and dimmable.

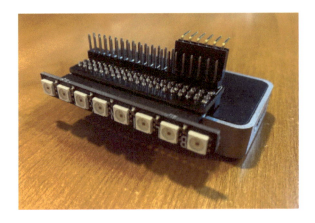

Fig. 4: LED Bar and 6-pin Right-angle Header attached to two GPIO Headers Split from Raspberry Pi (front view)

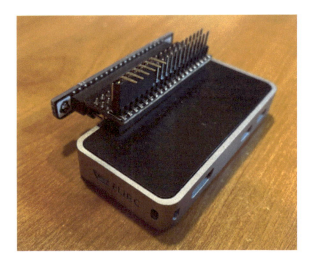

Fig. 5: LED Bar and 6-pin Right-angle Header attached to two GPIO Headers Split from Raspberry Pi (back view)

Blinkt! has 2x20 GPIO sockets (holes); it can sit directly on top of Raspberry Pi's GPIO header. Although it sits on the GPIO header, Blinkt! actually uses three GPIO pins only [2]:

- 5V power pin (physical pin #4)
- GPIO 23 (physical pin #16)
- GPIO 24 (physical pin #18)

Therefore, you can access the rest of the GPIO pins at the same time as using Blinkt! by splitting Raspberry Pi's GPIO header to two separate headers. Connect a GPIO splitter to Raspberry Pi's GPIO header, and plug Blinkt! into one of the two headers (Figs. 4 and 5). Make sure to plug in Blinkt! in the correct way [1]. The other header will be used in the next section to wire an accelerometer.

Attach Raspberry Pi to the head of the skateboard with a velcro strip (Fig. 1). Attach a portable charger to the skateboard with velcro as well, and power Raspberry Pi with a Micro USB cable (Fig. 1).

1.2.4 Connecting an Accelerometer to a Raspberry Pi

Glow in the Dark Skateboard uses the LIS3DH accelerometer. Plug a JST SH (or STEMMA QT) cable to the left connector of LIS3DH, which is circled in red in Fig. 6.

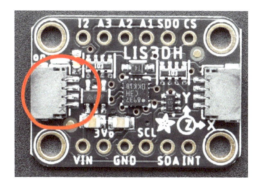

Fig. 6: LIS3DH Accelerometer

Plug a 6-pin right-angle GPIO header into the (top left) 3.3V, GPIO 2 (SDA1), GPIO 3 (SCL1), GPIO 4, GND and GPIO 7 pins (Fig. 5). Then, wire an accelerometer to 4 of them as shown in Fig. 7.

Screw the accelerometer onto a mounting plate, and attach the plate to the skateboard with a velcro strip (Fig. 1). Make sure that the accelerometer's left connector points to the head of the skateboard. In LIS3DH, the X, Y and X axes are set up as shown in Fig. 8. Glow in the Dark Skateboard assumes the X axis faces the direction that the skateboard goes.

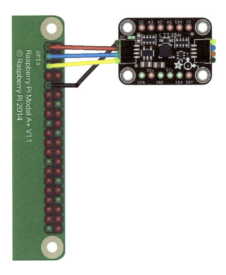

Fig. 7: Wiring of LIS3DH Accelerometer

Fig. 8: Sensing Axes of LIS3DH Accelerometer

1.3 Software Development

Glow in the Dark Skateboard runs Python code in Raspberry Pi to continuously sense the orientation (pitch angle) of the skateboard and flash LED lights. This section describes how to set up and run the Python code with the Blinkt! LED bar and LIS3DH accelerometer.

1.3.1 Installing Drivers for LED Bar and Accelerometer

This section explains how to make Blinkt! and LIS3DH accessible from Python. First, turn on a Raspberry Pi and update its operating system by running the following commands one by one on a Terminal.

- `sudo apt update -y`
- `sudo apt full-upgrade -y`

Then, run the following command to make Blinkt! ready to be used.

- `curl https://get.pimoroni.com/blinkt | bash`

See [3] for the reference manual of Blinkt!

In order to make LIS3DH ready to be used, enable I2C communication first with the Raspberry Pi Configuration settings. Then, run the following command on a Terminal.

- `i2cdetect -y 1`

LIS3DH is ready to communicate with Raspberry Pi through I2C, if you see "18" in the Terminal as shown in Fig. 9.

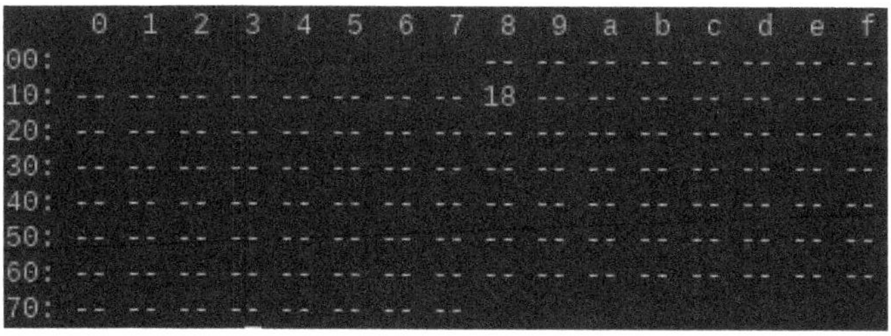

Fig. 9: Output of the i2cdetect Command

The next step is to download `lis3dh.py` from the "code" folder at [4] and run it when the skateboard is level. You can confirm that LIS3DH is running properly if you see an output like this.

```
LIS3DH configured with addr=0x18, sensing scale=±2g.
g: (0.052734375, 0.0390625, 0.9892578125)
m/s^2: (0.51711328125, 0.38304687499999995, 9.815576171875)
Pitch (degrees): -2.621751414971051 Roll (degrees): 3.01572138607504
```

Make sure that the reported pitch angle is close enough to 0, which means the skateboard is detected to be level. If the pitch is far from 0, double check if the accelerometer is attached to the skateboard as instructed earlier.

1.3.2 Python Code

Glow in the Dark Skateboard runs the following Python code, which is available as **orange-teal-fade-rainbow.py** in the "code" folder at [4]. Place this code and **lis3dh.py** in the same folder.

```python
import blinkt, time, math
from colorzero import Color, Hue
from lis3dh import LIS3DH

sensor = LIS3DH()
orange = Color(255, 0, 0) + Hue(deg=10)
teal = orange + Hue(deg=180)
red = Color(255, 0, 0)

def fadeInOut(color):
    x = 0
    while x < 1:
        blinkt.set_all(color.rgb_bytes[0],
                       color.rgb_bytes[1],
                       color.rgb_bytes[2], x)
        blinkt.show()
        time.sleep(0.01)
        x = x + 0.1
    x = 1
    while x > 0:
        blinkt.set_all(color.rgb_bytes[0],
                       color.rgb_bytes[1],
                       color.rgb_bytes[2], x)
        blinkt.show()
        time.sleep(0.01)
        x = x - 0.1
    x = 0

def rainbowBlink(color):
    i = 0
    while i <= 7 :
        blinkt.set_pixel(i, color.rgb_bytes[0],
                            color.rgb_bytes[1],
                            color.rgb_bytes[2], 1)
        color = color + Hue(deg=45)
        i = i + 1
    for x in range(5):
        blinkt.show()
        time.sleep(0.1)
        blinkt.clear()

def findPitch():
    x, y, z = sensor.readG()
    pitch, roll = sensor.pitchRoll(x, y, -z)
```

10

```
    pitch = math.degrees(pitch)
    return pitch

while True:
    try:
        pitch = findPitch()
        if pitch >= 5 or pitch <= -5:
            rainbowBlink(red)
        else:
            fadeInOut(orange)
            fadeInOut(teal)
    except KeyboardInterrupt:
        break
blinkt.clear()
blinkt.show()
```

1.3.3 Calculating the Pitch Angle of the Skateboard

Glow in the Dark Skateboard senses its orientation (e.g. level, upward or downward) to determine the LED bar's lighting pattern. It calculates the pitch angle as its orientation. The pitch angle is the angle between the horizontal ground surface and the base of the skateboard (θ in Fig. 10). Note that the X axis faces the direction that the skateboard goes. Therefore, when the pitch angle is close to zero, the skateboard is level. When it is positive, the skateboard is upward. It is downward when it is negative.

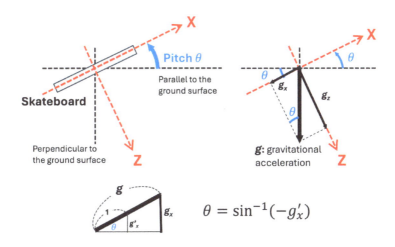

Fig. 10: Calculation of the Pitch Angle

The pitch angle is calculated with a formula that describes the relationship between the angle (θ) and the x-component of the gravitational acceleration. In Fig. 10, the gravitational acceleration is denoted by g, and its x-component is denoted by g_x. The formula is derived as follows. Looking at Fig. 10, the pitch angle θ is congruent to the vertical angle and the angle of the right triangle with the leg g_x. The right triangle, as shown at the left bottom of Fig. 10, has the hypotenuse of g and the leg g_x. Inside of this triangle, a similar triangle can be drawn with the hypotenuse being 1 and the leg being g_x'. As a result, $g_x' = \sin\theta$. g_x' is negated in the formula because the accelerometer reports g_x as a negative value.

In the Python code, the function `findPitch()` returns the pitch of the skateboard. In `findPitch()`, x-, y- and z-components of the gravitational acceleration are measured with the function `readG()` of `LIS3DH`. Then, the pitch angle is calculated with the function `pitchRoll()` of `LIS3DH` and converted from radians to degrees with the function `math.degrees()`.

1.3.4 Finding Complementary Colors and Rainbow Colors

Glow in the Dark Skateboard fades in and out of orange and its complementary color, teal blue, on the LED bar when its orientation is level. Orange is chosen because it matches the EL wire's color. You can change this choice if you use a different color for the EL wire.

Complementary colors are a pair of colors that work together by making the other brighter. When placed next to each other, they create the strongest contrast for the two colors and look vibrant together. They are on opposite sides of a color wheel, which organizes color hues around a circle and shows various relationships among them (Fig. 11). When the red color (R: 255, G: 0, B: 0) is placed at 0 degree (east), its complementary color, light blue, is at 180 degrees (west).

Glow in the Dark Skateboard uses the `colorzero` module [5] to pick up and adjust colors for LED lights. In the Python code, the following part sets up an orange color at 10 degrees counterclockwise from the red color (R: 255, G: 0, B: 0). Then, its complementary color is determined at 180 degrees from the orange color. It results in teal blue.

```
orange = Color(255, 0, 0) + Hue(deg=10)
teal = orange + Hue(deg=180)
```

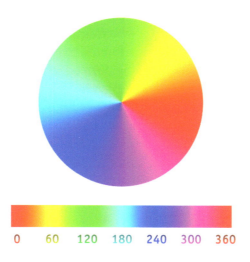

Fig. 11: Color Wheel

Glow in the Dark Skateboard also flashes rainbow colors on the LED bar when its orientation is upward or downward. Since the LED bar contains 8 lights, the rainbow colors are determined by equally dividing the color wheel into 8 parts. Since 360 degrees divided by 8 is 45, each color is 45 degrees away from each other. Starting at 0 degree, which is red, the next color is orange at 45 degrees, the third color is yellow at 90 degrees, etc. In the Python code, the function `rainbowBlink()` sets those 8 colors for the 8 LED lights and blinks them 5 times.

Currently, Glow in the Dark Skateboard considers that it is level when its pitch angle is in between -5 degrees and 5 degrees. It considers it is upward or downward when its pitch is higher than 5 degrees or lower than -5 degrees. These settings can be changed in an infinite loop at the bottom of the code.

1.4 Future Directions

Glow in the Dark Skateboard can be extended in many ways. One route is to focus on the health/fitness aspect of skateboarding. It is possible to detect when the skateboard moves by sensing acceleration over the x-axis because it indicates the force that a skateboarder applies to the skateboard with his/her foot. Therefore, the duration of a skateboarding session can be estimated. With extra inputs such as the skateboarder's weight and a skateboarding MET (metabolic equivalent) value, it is possible to estimate how many calories the rider has burned in the session. One MET is defined as 1 kcal/kg/hour and is roughly equivalent to the energy expenditure of sitting quietly. MET values of 5.0 and 8.0 are estimated for general (moderate-effort) and competitive (vigorous-effort) skateboarding, respectively [6, 7, 8].

To add on to the safety aspect, a motion sensor and an ultrasonic distance sensor can be added to the skateboard. They can monitor the surrounding condition to detect other road users (e.g. cars, bikers and pedestrians) and help avoid sudden curbs or bumps on the sidewalk. For safety precaution, the sensors can trigger a sound or visual warning to alert the skateboarder of the potential safety hazard.

1.5 Conclusion

This project delivers a technology hack to make skateboarding more fun and safer. It turns a traditional skateboard to be futuristic and smart with a Raspberry Pi computer and its peripheral components. Python code runs on the Raspberry Pi to control those peripherals. You can find the code and demo videos at [4].

References

[1] https://shop.pimoroni.com/products/blinkt

[2] https://pinout.xyz/pinout/blinkt

[3] http://docs.pimoroni.com/blinkt/

[4] https://github.com/HSSBoston/skateboard

[5] https://colorzero.readthedocs.io/

[6] https://pacompendium.com/sports/

[7] Ainsworth BE, Herrmann SD, Jacobs Jr. DR, Whitt-Glover MC, Tudor-Locke C. A brief history of the Compendium of Physical Activities. Journal of Sport and Health Science, 2024;13(1): 3-5.

[8] Herrmann SD, Willis EA, Ainsworth BE, Barreira TV, Hastert M, Kracht CL, Schuna Jr. JM, Cai Z, Quan M, Tudor-Locke C, Whitt-Glover MC, Jacobs DR. 2024 Adult Compendium of Physical Activities: A third update of the energy costs of human activities. Journal of Sport and Health Science, 2024;13(1): 6-12.

Biography

Hanna Suzuki is a 9th grader who loves reading, music, playing tennis, camping, and hanging out with her friends. She is a founding organizer of two international hackathons: PhysTech and AnimalHack. She has experienced coding with Lego WeDo, Scratch and Squeak Smalltalk since she was a kindergarten student. Most of her recent projects use Python and Raspberry Pi. She is a Python Certified Entry-level Programmer. Hanna won two Global Championships (2022 and 2021) and a Global Finalist Honorable Mention (2023) in the NASA International Space Apps Challenge. She was selected as one of 10 national finalists (2024) and the Massachusetts state merit winner (2023) in the 3M Young Scientist Challenge. Hanna has been active to serve regional, nation-wide, and international K-12 communities by sharing her skills and experience in coding and electronics. Her service was recognized by the President of the United States, and she received Gold Medals of the President's Volunteer Service Award in 2023 and 2024. Hanna also studies piano at the New England Conservatory Preparatory School and has been invited to the Carnegie Hall for her recitals eight times.

Chapter 2

Fishing Tracker

Rei Nagata

Rye High School
Rye, NY 10580, USA

Abstract

This project develops a device that can help you know
when it is best to go fishing. It is a Raspberry Pi-powered system, called the Fishing Tracker, which displays important factors for fishing such as tide times,
air temperature and humidity. It runs Python code to
download those data from online services and display
them on a digital message board. This chapter describes how to assemble and use the Fishing Tracker.

2.1 Introduction

Fishing takes up a huge amount of time and lots of dedication. Although fishing itself is fun, there are tons of problems when fishing.
The most major one is ending up with no catches as all the preparation
and commitment are not paid off.

This project builds a Raspberry Pi-powered system, called the Fishing
Tracker, which is designed to display various environmental factors
that impact fishing results such as tide times, air temperature, humidity, seawater temperature and wind speed. Currently, the Fishing
Tracker displays three of them: tide times, air temperature and humidity. It runs Python code to download tide time forecasts from the National Oceanic and Atmospheric Administration (NOAA) and weather
forecasts from OpenWeatherMap. The Python code can display the
forecasts for two locations in the US on a digital message board
(128x64 LED panel). Fig. 1 shows an example data display on the
LED panel.

This chapter explains how to assemble hardware components and configure Python code for running the Fishing Tracker properly. It also describes how to use and potentially extend it.

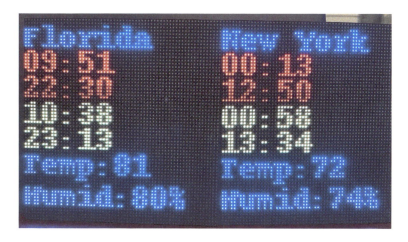

Fig. 1: An Example Data Display of the Fishing Tracker. High-tide times (today's tides in red and tomorrow's tides in yellow), air temperature and humidity in Florida and New York.

2.2 Use Cases

This project is useful for anyone who loves going out fishing. Here is one possible case that this project could be used in. Let's say that you just bought a very expensive rod and very expensive lures. You wanted to go try it out so you went to the nearest shore to try and catch some fish. You are expecting to catch a lot of fish because you bought some very expensive stuff. However, there is a huge problem. Even with your expensive gear, you still can't catch any fish at all. Your excitement of being able to catch more fish has turned into frustration and anger. This project could be used to solve these problems as well. Since this project is able to display and provide you with information on the best time to go fishing, you can use the project to then counter these problems. Now that you have this information using the project, it doesn't even matter if you have the best gear or not.

Also, the Fishing Tracker may be customized depending on what kind of information you want to know about and you can change the color and size of the writings. In my case, I displayed the time of the high tides, the humidity, and the temperature.

2.3 Hardware Setup

This section explains how you can build the Fishing Tracker yourself. Here is a list of all the necessary parts:

- Raspberry Pi 3 Model A+ & MicroSD card (1x)
- Raspberry Pi Adapter (1x)
- RGB LED Matrix Panels 64x64 (2x)
- Gray Ribbon Cables(2x)
- Jumper Wire Metal to Metal (1x)
- Power Cable (1x)
- Screw Terminal Block (1x)
- Power Supply Cable (1x)

2.3.1 Connect the Raspberry Pi and the Adapter

You will plug the power supply cable into the Raspberry Pi. Connect the adapter by first, finding the GPIO pins on the Raspberry Pi. Then, you should be able to find the black block with many holes that the GPIO Pin goes into. You must attach the adapter onto the Raspberry Pi the right way or else it would not work. It should fit perfectly and should look like Fig. 2.

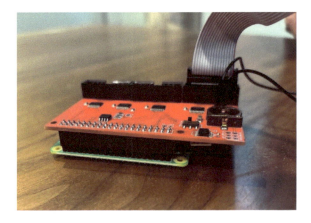

Fig. 2: The Raspberry Pi and LED Panel Adapter

On the Raspberry Pi adapter, you will also see three black boxes with several pins in them. You will then take the gray ribbon cable and attach it to the black box on the left side of the adapter. This gray ribbon cable will be used to attach the 2 LED panels to the adapter.

2.3.2 Prepare the Power Supply Cable

Connect both parts of the power supply cable. First, plug one end into an outlet and the other to a screw terminal block. Then, take the plastic end of the power cable (not the power supply cable) and plug it into the LED panel's power cable connector which is in the middle box of the LED panel. After, the metal side of the power cable will go into the screw terminal block. However, be careful and make sure that the red wire goes into the + side of the screw terminal block and the black side goes into the - side of the screw terminal block. If you accidentally switch these up, you can just fix it but if you don't realize it beforehand, you might end up getting confused later on when the LED panel is not displaying anything.

2.3.3 Wiring on the Adapter

First, get the jumper wire. Then, you will find eight holes on the adapter and on that two of them should be labeled #E and #P8 on the bottom row. These two holes are where you will put the jumper wires.

2.3.4 Connect the 2 LED Panels

The next step is wiring the two LED panels to the Raspberry Pi. You will then take the other side of the gray ribbon cable that is connected to the adapter and plug it into the Input connector (left). You will take another gray ribbon cable and plug it into the output connector (right) and the other side of that cable into the input connector of the second LED panel. (Fig. 3).

After following all of these steps, you should be able to work it after completing the codes. It is sometimes really hard to stay organized and keep track of everything. There are times that some parts detach or come off so you should always recheck that everything's in its place first before running the codes. If you do run the code when there is something wrong with it, an error might pop up which could also confuse you. To prevent any errors or mistakes from occurring, you should always check again that everything is in place. If you complete all these steps that are instructed, you should be ready now to type in the codes and finish this project. (Fig. 4).

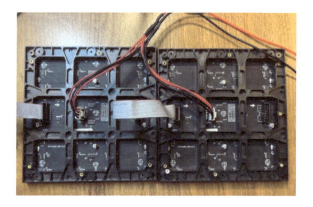

Fig. 3: The Gray Ribbon Cables connecting the 2 LED Panels

Fig. 4: Completed Setup

2.4 Coding

The Fishing Tracker runs the following Python code.

```python
from noaa_coops import getHighTideTimesToday
from noaa_coops import getHighTideTimesTomorrow
import time, sys
from rgbmatrix import RGBMatrix, RGBMatrixOptions
from PIL import Image, ImageDraw, ImageFont
from openweather import *


stationId = 8723214


highTideTimesToday = getHighTideTimesToday(stationId)
print(highTideTimesToday)
print(highTideTimesToday[0])
if len(highTideTimesToday) == 2:
    print(highTideTimesToday[1])


highTideTimesTomorrow = getHighTideTimesTomorrow(stationId)
print(highTideTimesTomorrow)

print(highTideTimesTomorrow[0])
if len(highTideTimesTomorrow) == 2:
    print(highTideTimesTomorrow[1])

stationIdtwo = 8516945


highTideTimesTodayn = getHighTideTimesToday(stationIdtwo)
print(highTideTimesTodayn)
print(highTideTimesTodayn[0])


highTideTimesTomorrown = getHighTideTimesTomorrow(stationIdtwo)
print(highTideTimesTomorrown)
print(highTideTimesTomorrown[0])


stationIdthree = 9410840


highTideTimesTodayt = getHighTideTimesToday(stationIdthree)
print(highTideTimesTodayt)
print(highTideTimesTodayt[0])


highTideTimesTomorrowt = getHighTideTimesTomorrow(stationIdthree)
print(highTideTimesTomorrowt)
print(highTideTimesTomorrowt[0])


weatherApiKey = ""


cityName1 = "Rye"
stateCode1 = "NY"
weatherData = getUsWeather(cityName1, stateCode1,
                           weatherApiKey, unit="imperial")
temp, feelsLike, humidity = getCurrentTempHumidity(weatherData)
RyeTemp = str(temp)
RyeHumidity = str(humidity)
print("Temp (F): " + str(temp) + ", Feels like (F): " + \
      str(feelsLike) + ", Humidity (%): " + str(humidity))


cityName2 = "Miami"
```

```
countryCode2 = "US"
weatherData2 = getIntlWeather(cityName2, countryCode2,
                              weatherApiKey, unit="imperial")
temp, feelsLike, humidity = getCurrentTempHumidity(weatherData2)
MiamiTemp = str(temp)
MiamiHumidity = str(humidity)
print("Temp (F): " + str(temp) + ", Feels like (F): " + \
        str(feelsLike) + ", Humidity (%): " + str(humidity))


options = RGBMatrixOptions()
options.cols = 128
options.rows = 64
options.parallel = 1
options.gpio_slowdown = 3
options.drop_privileges=False


panelImageFileName = "panel.jpg"
imageWidth = 128
imageHeight = 64


image = Image.new("RGB", (imageWidth, imageHeight), (0, 0, 0))
draw = ImageDraw.Draw(image)
font = ImageFont.load_default()


draw.text((0,  8),highTideTimesToday[0], fill=(255, 0, 0), font=font)
draw.text((0, 16),highTideTimesToday[1], fill=(255, 0, 0), font=font)
draw.text((0, 24),highTideTimesTomorrow[0], fill=(255, 255, 0),
                  font=font)
draw.text((0, 32),highTideTimesTomorrow[1], fill=(255, 255, 0),
                  font=font)
draw.text((0,  40),"Temp:", fill=(0, 0, 255), font=font)
draw.text((0,  50),"Humid:", fill=(0, 0, 255), font=font)
draw.text((64, 40),"Temp:", fill=(0, 0, 255), font=font)
draw.text((64, 50),"Humid:", fill=(0, 0, 255), font=font)
draw.text((98, 50),RyeHumidity, fill=(0, 0, 255), font=font)
draw.text((92, 40),RyeTemp, fill=(0, 0, 255), font=font)
draw.text((34, 50),MiamiHumidity, fill=(0, 0, 255), font=font)
draw.text((28, 40),MiamiTemp, fill=(0, 0, 255), font=font)
draw.text((64,  0),"New York", fill=(0, 0, 255), font=font)
draw.text((0,   0),"Florida", fill=(0, 0, 225), font=font)
draw.text((64,  8),highTideTimesTodayn[0], fill=(255, 0, 0),
                  font=font)
draw.text((64, 16),highTideTimesTodayn[1], fill=(255, 0, 0),
                  font=font)
draw.text((64, 24),highTideTimesTomorrown[0], fill=(255, 255, 0),
                  font=font)
draw.text((64, 32),highTideTimesTomorrown[1], fill=(255, 255, 0),
                  font=font)

matrix = RGBMatrix(options = options)
matrix.SetImage(image)


while True:
    try:
        time.sleep(100)
    except KeyboardInterrupt:
        break
```

The `stationId` and `stationIdtwo` variables are expected to have the station IDs that are used by the Tides and Currents Service of the National Oceanic and Atmospheric Administration (NOAA). Currently, they have the station IDs for Virginia Key, FL, (8723214) and Kings Point, NY, (8516945). You can use other stations/locations if you want. Search other stations and their IDs at `https://tidesandcurrents.noaa.gov/` and set them to `stationId` and `stationIdtwo`.

The `weatherApiKey` variable is expected to have an API key to download weather forecasts from the OpenWeatherMap service. Create your own API key for OpenWeatherMap at `https://openweathermap.org/` and assign it to the variable.

2.5 Future Steps

There are still some parts that can be added to improve the Fishing Tracker. The project right now is still not what I wanted it to be from the beginning. The goal from the start was to be able to create a new equation that can give me the probability of catching some fish that day using all the data and information that is collected from 2 websites. However right now, the project is only able to display the time of the high tides, the humidity, and the temperature which is not enough information to create a working and reliable equation. Therefore, I am also trying to make it so that this project is able to collect and display even more information such as the weather, the wind speed, and the seawater temperature.

2.6 Conclusion

There is nothing more frustrating than spending a lot of time fishing and going home empty handed. To prevent or at least lessen the chance of this happening, this project offers you the Fishing Tracker so that you will be able to tell when it is best to go out fishing. Since the most important aspect of fishing is the time that you go, the Fishing Tracker can be really helpful in these situations. I hope you can find success in completing this project on your own!

Biography

Rei Nagata is a 9th grader who loves sports, coding and animals. He plays on a club team in the Major League Soccer NEXT league, which is the highest-level competition platform in the US and Canada. He regularly plays against professional academy teams such as NYCFC. In 2024, his team made it to the top 8 worldwide in the Gothia Cup, which is often referred to as the Youth World Cup. Rei also plays baseball as a pitcher and an outfielder. He enjoys fishing and skiing as well. Rei has a strong interest in integrating his physical activity with computer science. He is a co-founder of PhysTech and an organizer of AnimalHack 2024. His projects won the Silver Prize at AnimalHack 2023 and the Rising Talent Award in PhysTech 2024. Rei is a Certified Entry-Level Python Programmer.

Chapter 3

Fencing Priority Referee: A Wearable Sensor for Data-centric Priority Judgment

Nikichi Tsuchida

Winchester High School
Winchester, MA 01890, USA

Abstract

This project develops a lightweight and wearable device for fencing, called the Fencing Priority Referee (FPR). The FPR is designed to help identify which fencer deserves "priority," or "right of way" to score a point when two fencers land an attack simultaneously. It is built with a Raspberry Pi computer and an accelerometer to track a fencer's body movement and detect the moment of attack. Its threshold-based attack detection algorithm is implemented in Python and evaluated with the datasets recorded in a controlled environment and real bouts.

3.1 Introduction

Fencing is a sport that has been known for its mesmerizing swordplay over the centuries. Although it may look like simple sword fighting, there is complexity in the game of fencing as it is often referred to as "physical chess." It requires mental discipline and strategic decisions, responding to and initiating attacks in a very closed space.

Fencing is split into three sections: *foil*, *sabre* and *epee*. Although they share the primary objective of the game – hitting the target area on an opponent's body with a blade before being hit [1], they employ different rules with different blade types and require different strategies and tactics. This gives depth to the game of fencing.

In foil fencing, fencers use a weapon called a "foil," which is a flexible sword-like object that is 110 cm or under in total length and weighs 500 grams or below [2]. When foil fencing, fencers can only score a point if the tip of their foil hits the opponent's torso [3]. Similarly in epee fencing, fencers have to hit their opponents with the tip of their sword for the point to count; however, they do not have to hit the opponent's torso as the target in epee is the whole body [3]. Fencers in epee fencing utilize a weapon called an "epee" which has a stiffer blade than foil but is still quite flexible, it is also the heaviest weapon out of the three types of fencing, resulting in epee fencing being slower than foil and sabre [2]. As you might have guessed by now, in sabre fencing fencers use a weapon called a "sabre", sabre is unique to foil and epee as it commonly has a cutting edge, resulting in sabre fencers being able to score points by hitting opponents with the edge of their sabre and not only the tip [4]. Sabres are shorter than the foil and epee, enabling sabre fencers to be faster paced, but the target only being above the waist of the opponent slows the fencing style from going too fast [2].

This project focuses on foil fencing and addresses a common issue in foil fencing practice: judging who had priority, or right of way, to score a point when two fencers hit each other simultaneously. This judgment is made based on several factors such as parrying, reposte, point in line, and attacks on the blade. If the fencers did not have these interactions, priority is given to the one who initiated the attack earlier. In practice sessions, it is often hard for fencers to visually make this judgment. They need to have a conversation like "Was that your point or mine?" again and again.

This project proposes and evaluates a wearable device that tracks the body movement of a fencer and detects the moment of attack. Built with a Raspberry Pi and an accelerometer, the proposed device, called the Fencing Priority Referee (FPR), is attached to the lower back of a fencer with a belt. It is as lightweight as 199 grams. The FPR runs Python programs to record the acceleration of body movement every 0.01 second and detect when forward acceleration exceeds a certain threshold. The ultimate goal of this project is to have two fencers wear the FPRs in a bout, track their body movement and help them judge which one had priority when they land an attack simultaneously.

This chapter describes how to assemble hardware components to build the FPR and how to configure its Python programs for collecting, storing and visualizing acceleration data. Its attack detection algorithm is evaluated through empirical experiments.

3.2 Assembling the Fencing Priority Referee (FPR)

This section explains the overall system structure of the FPR and provides instructions to replicate it.

3.2.1 Hardware Components

The following components are required to build the FPR.

- 1x Raspberry Pi Zero 2 W: The device will be the "brains" of the FPR and will be running codes. ASIN: B09LTDQY2Z.

- 1x SanDisk 32GB Ultra microSDHC UHS-I Memory Card: ASIN: B073JWXGNT.

- 1x Adafruit Swirly Aluminum Mounting Grid for 0.1" Spaced PCBs - 5x5: The product is used to maintain the main structure of the FPR. Adafruit Product ID: 5779.

- 1x Adafruit LIS3DH Triple-Axis Accelerometer: The accelerometer serves the purpose of detecting the acceleration of the fencer with the FPR. Adafruit Product ID: 2809.

- 1x STEMMA QT / Qwiic JST SH 4-pin Cable with Premium Female Sockets - 150mm Long: The cable allows for the connection between the Raspberry Pi and the accelerometer in the FPR. Adafruit Product ID: 4397.

- 1x Bewinner 2 x 20 Pins 2.54mm Pitch Female Pin Header: The pin header connects the accelerometer to the Raspberry Pi. ASIN: B07P57N3TZ.

- 1x Portable charger: The portable charger is needed to power the FPR. Any portable charger would work, however, it is recommended to use small and light chargers such as this. ASIN: B09BBCPC3X.

- 1x USB A to micro USB cable: The cable is used to connect the portable charger to the Raspberry Pi. Any USB A to micro USB cable would work, however, it is recommended to use cables long enough to reach the FPR but short enough to not be a hindrance such as this. ASIN: B0BHNVLW1Z.

- 1x Belt: The belt is used to secure the FPR onto the body of a fencer. This belt must be designed for additional holes to be punctured, such as this belt. ASIN: B01M8KIMS6.

- 1x Metric M2.5 Phillips Pan Head Nylon Screws Nut Washer Assortment Kit: The kit will be utilized to secure the accelerometer, belt, and Raspberry Pi onto the mounting grid. ASIN: B0BL3RW7PJ.

Note that ASINs are identification codes that can be used at `https://www.amazon.com` to find specific products. Adafruit Product IDs can be used to identify products at `https://www.adafruit.com`.

3.2.2 Enabling I2C

Raspberry Pi interacts with LIS3DH with a communication mechanism called I2C. Thus, you need to enable I2C first. Click the Raspberry Pi menu at the upper left corner of the Raspberry Pi screen, select "Preferences," and then select "Raspberry Pi Configuration." In a window that pops up, select the "Interfaces" tab and turn I2C enabled there. When asked if you want to reboot, select Yes.

3.2.3 Connecting LIS3DH to Raspberry Pi

Plug a right-angle header into the Raspberry Pi's GPIO header, and connect a QT cable to one of the two connectors of LIS3DH (Fig. 1). Then, wire LIS3DH to GPIO pins as follows (Fig. 1):

- Red wire to a 3.3V pin
- Blue wire to the GPIO 2 (SDA1) pin
- Yellow wire to the GPIO 3 (SCK1) pin
- Black wire to a ground pin

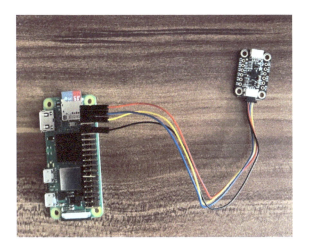

Fig. 1: Wiring of LIS3DH

To confirm the connection between the Raspberry Pi and LIS3DH, run `i2cdetect -y 1` on a Terminal. LIS3DH is ready to be used if the command outputs "18."

3.2.4 Testing LIS3DH

Run the following Python program to see if LIS3DH works properly.

```python
import time
from lis3dh import LIS3DH

sensor = LIS3DH()
while True:
    try:
        x, y, z = sensor.readG()
        print(x, y, z)
        time.sleep(1)
    except KeyboardInterrupt:
        break
```

This program initializes LIS3DH and reads data from it every second. The data's unit is *g*. (1*g* indicates the gravitational acceleration.) This program runs with an infinite loop; stop running it with Ctrl-C.

Fig. 2: Sensing Axes of LIS3DH

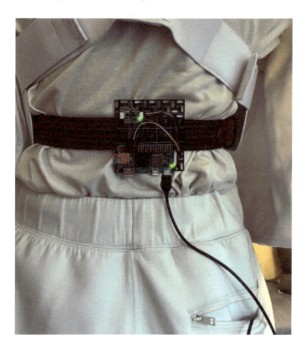

Fig. 3: FPR on the back of a fencer

Note that the x-, y- and z-axes are configured in LIS3DH as shown in Fig. 2. When the x- and y-axes are parallel to the ground surface and the accelerometer faces up, the z-axis points to the ground. As a result, the accelerometer reports the z value of +1g. The x and y values are zeros. Similarly, when the x-axis is perpendicular to the ground surface, the x value is reported to be +1g. The remaining two values are zeros. When the y-axis is perpendicular to the ground, the y value becomes +1g, and the remaining two values become zeros.

3.2.5 Attaching the FPR to a Fencer

Screw the Raspberry Pi and LIS3DH onto a mounting plate. Then, make holes on a belt and screw the mounting plate to the belt. Wrap the belt around a fencer's lower back and fasten it. Put a portable charger in the back pocket for supplying power to the Raspberry Pi. Fig. 3 shows the complete setup of the FPR.

Fig. 4: Fencer Standing Still

Fig. 5: Fencer Lunging

3.3 Attack Detection

This section describes how to collect, store and visualize acceleration data with the FPR. It also presents how to configure and run the FPR's attack detection algorithm. The detection algorithm is evaluated with the datasets collected in a controlled environment and real bouts.

3.3.1 Data Collection in a Controlled Environment

To run and evaluate the FPR's attack detection algorithm, a controlled environment is defined to collect datasets. In a single data collection cycle, a fencer with the FPR stands still for about 5 seconds (Fig. 4). Then, the fencer suddenly moves forward to lunge (Fig. 5). The following Python program is used to read acceleration data from LIS3DH and save them in a CSV file.

```python
import csv, time
from iotutils import getCurrentTimeStamp
from lis3dh import LIS3DH

sensor = LIS3DH()
accelData = []
initialTime = time.time()

while True:
    try:
        x, y, z = sensor.readG()
        currentTime = time.time()
        elapsedTime = round(currentTime - initialTime, 3)
        accelData.append([elapsedTime, x, y, z])
        time.sleep(0.01)
    except KeyboardInterrupt:
        break

timeStamp = getCurrentTimeStamp()
fileName = "accel-" + timeStamp + ".csv"
with open(fileName, "w") as f:
    writer = csv.writer(f)
    writer.writerow(["Elapsed time (s)", "X (G)", "Y (G)", "Z (G)"])
    writer.writerows(accelData)
print(fileName + " saved.")
```

This program reads acceleration over x-, y- and z-axes every 0.01 second. It records a timestamp for each acceleration read. The timestamp is expressed as an elapsed time since the current data collection started. When acceleration reading is terminated with Ctrl-C, this program saves all acceleration and timestamp data into a CSV file.

3.3.2 Attack Detection in a Controlled Environment

The FPR requires the **matplotlib** module to run its attack detection algorithm and visualize detection results. Install it by running the following commands one by one on a Terminal.

- `sudo pip3 install matplotlib`
- `sudo pip3 install numpy --upgrade`
- `sudo apt install libatlas-base-dev -y`
- `sudo apt install libopenblas-dev -y`

The following program reads acceleration data in a CSV file, performs attack detection and visualizes the moment of attack in a time series graph. The FPR determines the moment of attack by identifying when forward acceleration (positive acceleration over the z-axis) exceeds a certain threshold. The default threshold is set to be +1.0 g. See the red line in the program.

```python
import matplotlib.pyplot as plt
import csv, numpy as np

inputFileName = "FILENAME"
accelThreshold = 1.0
elapsedTimeList = []
zAccelList = []

with open(inputFileName, "r") as f:
    reader = csv.reader(f)
    next(reader)
    for row in reader:
        elapsedTimeList.append( float(row[0]) )
        zAccelList.append( float(row[3]) )

for i in range(len(zAccelList)):
    if zAccelList[i] > accelThreshold:
        changePointIndex = i
        break

channgePointTime = elapsedTimeList[changePointIndex]
changePointAccel = zAccelList[changePointIndex]

print("Change point index", changePointIndex)
print("Change point time", channgePointTime)
print("Change point accel", changePointAccel)

plt.plot(elapsedTimeList, zAccelList)
plt.vlines(channgePointTime, 2, -2, colors="red", linestyle="dashed",
linewidth=2)

plt.xlabel("Elapsed Time (s)", fontsize=14)
plt.ylabel("Acceleration (g)", fontsize=14)
plt.grid(True)
plt.show()
```

Of a series of acceleration data in a CSV file, this program identifies a particular data point that exceeds the threshold. The data point is called a "change point." This program outputs the change point's acceleration value (in g) and timestamp. (See the blue lines in the above program.)

Fig. 6 shows the graphs that this program generates for the 13 datasets captured in the controlled environment. In each graph, the x- and y-axis denote elapsed time (in second) and forward acceleration (in g). A blue line indicates how forward acceleration changes over time. For approximately five seconds in the beginning, it is nearly zero because the fencer stands still. Then, it spikes when the fencer lunges. A red vertical (dotted) line indicates where a change point is.

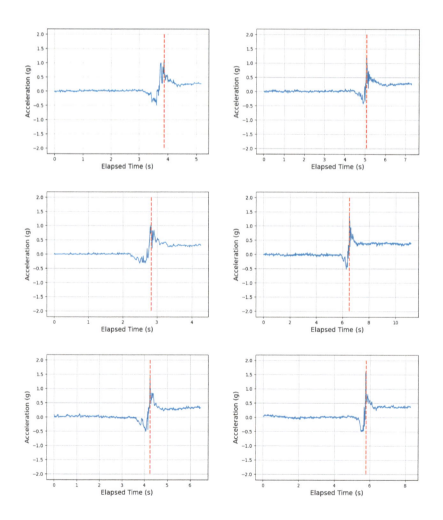

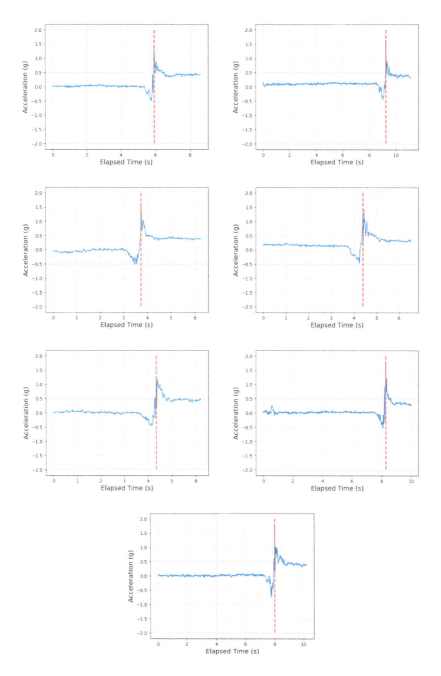

Fig. 6: Attack Detection Results in a Controlled Environment

As illustrated in each graph of Fig. 6, the FPR successfully detects the moment of attack. The acceleration threshold of +1.0 g works for the controlled environment.

3.3.3 Attack Detection in Real Fencing Bouts

In addition to a controlled environment, the FPR is evaluated in real bouts as well. Fig. 7 shows the datasets recorded in three bouts. In each of them, a fencer starts to move immediately after a data collection session starts and keeps moving while attacking throughout the session. A red vertical (dotted) line indicates a change point that the FPR determines. An orange line indicates the actual moment of attack. Therefore, if a red line overlaps an orange line, the FPR correctly detects an attack. Otherwise, the FPR identifies a change point where a fencer actually does not initiate an attack. If an orange line is shown without a red line overlapped, the FPR fails to detect an attack.

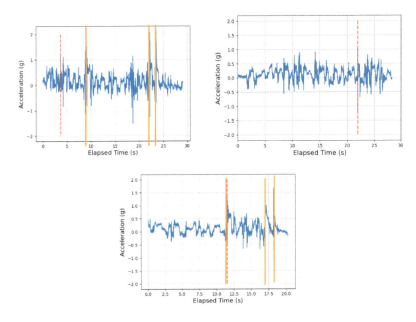

Fig. 7: Attack Detection in Real Fencing Bouts

In the first graph of Fig. 7, the FPR identifies a change point around the elapsed time of 4 seconds where the fencer moves forward but does not attack. It fails to detect three attacks afterwards. In the second graph, the FPR identifies a change point around the elapsed time of

22 seconds, which is not an attack. In the third graph, the FPR correctly identifies a change point around the elapsed time of 11.25 seconds; however, it fails to detect two attacks afterwards.

These false positives and negatives occur because the program in the previous section uses a relatively low acceleration threshold (+1.0 g) and looks for only one change point in a single bout. Therefore, it has been revised as follows by increasing the threshold and seeking multiple change points in a bout.

```python
import matplotlib.pyplot as plt
import csv

inputFileName = "FILENAME"
accelThreshold = 1.4
minInterval = 0.5
elapsedTimeList = []
zAccelList = []

with open(inputFileName, "r") as f:
    reader = csv.reader(f)
    next(reader)
    for row in reader:
        elapsedTimeList.append(float(row[0]))
        zAccelList.append(float(row[3]))

lastChangePointTime = -float('inf')

plt.plot(elapsedTimeList, zAccelList, label="Z Acceleration")

for i in range(len(zAccelList)):
    if zAccelList[i] > accelThreshold:
        changePointTime = elapsedTimeList[i]

        if changePointTime - lastChangePointTime >= minInterval:
            changePointAccel = zAccelList[i]
            print("Change point index", i)
            print("Change point time", changePointTime)
            print("Change point accel", changePointAccel)

            plt.vlines(changePointTime,
                       min(zAccelList), max(zAccelList),
                       colors="red", linestyle="dashed",
                       linewidth=2)
            lastChangePointTime = changePointTime

plt.xlabel("Elapsed Time (s)", fontsize=14)
plt.ylabel("Acceleration (g)", fontsize=14)
plt.grid(True)
plt.show()
```

This revised program uses a threshold of +1.4 g to reduce false positives. It also seeks multiple moments of attack to reduce false negatives. To avoid identifying multiple change points from a single attack, this program pauses attack detection for 0.5 second after identifying a change point. In general, it is very difficult for a fencer to execute two distinct strikes within 0.5 second.

Fig. 8 shows the results of the revised attack detection algorithm. In comparison to Fig. 7, it demonstrates that the revised algorithm successfully performs attack detection by eliminating false positive and negatives.

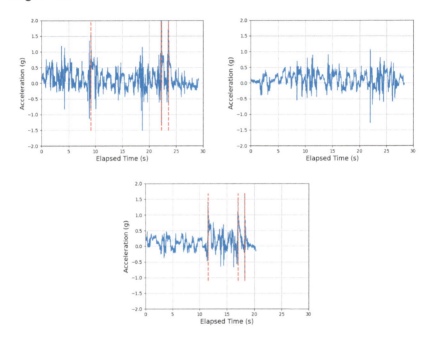

Fig. 8: Attack Detection with the Revised Algorithm in Real Fencing Bouts

3.4 Future Works

While the FPR was able to keep track of the acceleration of the fencer and notify when the fencer initiated an attack by using the acceleration threshold algorithm, there are several changes that could be made to further enhance the capabilities of the electronic referee.

One change would be to use a more precise algorithm than the threshold algorithm. Although the threshold algorithm can detect when a fencer has initiated an attack it is not too reliable. This was evident from how when the threshold algorithm was 1g, it detected a fast advancement and believed it to be an attack. In fencing there is variety in attacking and movement, some attacks could be slow and some movements may be quick, and determining what was movement and what was an attack in situations like this is where the threshold algorithm fails.

Another change would be implementing another accelerometer into the FPR in order for the electronic referee to track both of the fencers in a fencing bout instead of one. This enhancement will greatly benefit the FPR as it allows for two trackers to begin at the exact same time, and graph the two data on the same graph, making it apparent who initiated the attack.

3.5 Conclusion

This chapter reports the Fencing Priority Referee (FPR), a wearable device that assists fencers to determine who deserves a point when they strike each other simultaneously. It uses a Raspberry Pi and an accelerometer to track each fencer's body movement and detect the moment of attack. It leverages Python to perform a threshold-based algorithm for attack detection. The attack detection algorithm is empirically evaluated with the datasets recorded in a controlled environment and real bouts.

References

[1] Evangelista, Nick Forrest and Granet, Elijah. "fencing". *Encyclopedia Britannica*, 28 Feb. 2024, https://www.britannica.com/sports/fencing. Accessed 28 July 2024.
[2] *Rules for Competitions Book 3. Material Rules*, www.britishfencing.com/uploads/files/book_m_-_20151209.pdf. Accessed 28 July 2024.
[3] *Fencing Competition Types: Foil, Sabre, and Epee - ACTIVESG*, www.activesgcircle.gov.sg/learn/fencing/fencing-competition-types-foil-sabre-and-epee. Accessed 28 July 2024.

[4] *General Rules and Rules Common to the Three Weapons*, static.fie.org/uploads/18/92877-Technical%20rules%20ang.pdf. Accessed 28 July 2024.

Biography

Nikichi Tsuchida is a high school junior who enjoys physics, mathematics, and singing. Since he was an elementary school student, he has been passionate about choir and theater, performing on stage and volunteering at hospitals, churches, and English study workshops. Nikichi founded and has been leading the Physics Club in his high school. His love for physics bloomed when he wrote an essay about the double slit experiment for a middle school science class. He was instantly fascinated by the mind-boggling phenomena. Since then, he has been building his own Van de Graaff generator to conduct high-voltage experiments. He hopes to major in astrophysics and particle physics in the future. In his spare time, Nikichi enjoys fencing, mathematics, video games with friends, and pickling vegetables.

Chapter 4

Runs Created Value (RCV): A New Batting Performance Statistic in Baseball

Shun Nagata

Rye High School
Rye, NY 10580, USA

Abstract

This project proposes a new baseball statistic, called Runs Created Value (RCV), which indicates each batter's contribution to runs per at-bat. RCV is designed to quantify the overall offensive ability of a batter by integrating both positive and negative outcomes. This chapter calculates the RCV of all MLB batters in the 2024 season and analyzes statistical properties of RCV such as central tendency and distribution. This aids in predicting performance, comparing a player to others and to the whole league, and making decisions on team/lineup formation, scouting, and trading. This chapter also develops an Internet of Things (IoT) device that displays the top and bottom MLB batters in terms of RCV. It uses a Raspberry Pi computer to run Python code that downloads a stats dataset from the MLB API, calculates each batter's RCV and shows a sorted RCV result on an LED panel.

4.1 Introduction

In baseball, it is hard to find talented players solely by skimming through their stats. It is extremely challenging since it is difficult to figure out how impressive particular numbers are. In order to find

41

exceptional players, it is necessary to set criteria to properly assess the talent of the player. One method, which is the one that I used, is to take into account the trends of the whole league.

After contemplating what the best methods to indicate the data are, I eventually decided to utilize a boxplot and a histogram to display the data of the whole league and charts to display the data of individuals.

Furthermore, RCV properly measures both the positive and the negative outcomes of players' at bats and integrates them into one value. The formula of RCV is written in section 3.1.

The project idea that I decided to implement was "RCV Visualizer." It is essentially a tool that assists people in figuring out players with talent or evaluating players in comparison to the league.

4.2 Background

There are many existing MLB stat categories that quantify the run contribution of each player. Five of them are briefly described below.

4.2.1 On-Base Plus Slugging (OPS)

Formula: $OPS = OBP + SLG$

By combining On-Base Percentage (OBP) and Slugging (SLG), OPS attempts to determine the overall number that represents the batters' abilities to get on base and hit for extra bases. OPS of .800 or above is generally considered to be in the upper half of the league.

4.2.2 Weighted On-Base Average (wOBA)

Formula: $wOBA = (uBB\ Factor \times uBB + HBP\ Factor \times HBP + 1B\ Factor \times 1B + 2B\ Factor \times 2B + 3B\ Factor \times 3B + HR\ Factor \times HR)\ /\ (AB + BB - IBB + SF + HBP)$

The measurement of wOBA is based on the concept that not all hits have equal values. Other stats like Batting Average and On Base Percentage calculate all hits equally. On the other hand, wOBA combines various aspects of hitting into one and takes into account the value of each outcome. Additionally, the formula changes from year to year due to the factors.

4.2.3 Run Created (RC)

Formula: $RC = TB \times (H + BB) / (AB + BB)$

RC determines a player's offensive contribution. RC summarizes a player's offensive abilities in terms of total runs. The first part of the formula combines the player's ability to get on base with the ability to hit extra base hits, and the second part divides it by the total opportunities.

4.2.4 wRC (Weighted Runs Created)

Formula: $wRC = (((wOBA\text{-}League\ wOBA)/wOBA\ Scale)+(League\ R/PA)) \times PA$

wRC is an improvement on Runs Created. The purpose of the stat is still the same: To quantify a player's offensive contributions by measuring it in runs. There are two main advancements from Runs Created. First, wRC involves wOBA, which takes into account more factors such as sacrifice flies. Secondly, wRC is adjusted based on the league's offensive environment of the year.

4.2.5 Weighted Runs Created Plus (wRC+)

Formula: $wRC+ = (((wRAA/PA + League\ R/PA) + (League\ R/PA - Park\ Factor \times League\ R/PA))/ (AL\ or\ NL\ wRC/PA\ excluding\ pitchers)) \times 100$

wRC+ is a more standardized version of wRC. It measures how a player's wRC compares with the league after being adjusted based on park factors. League average is 100, and every point above 100 is a percentage above league average, and every point below 100 is a percentage point below league average. Each ballpark has different features. For instance, Coors Park is known to be a hitters' park, while T-Mobile park is pitcher friendly. In 2023, the frequency of players recording hits in Coors Park was 30% higher than that of T-Mobile Park.

4.3 The RCV Visualizer

Most of the RCV Visualizer system uses solely a single computer with a program called Thonny installed in it. (Fig. 1) The LED panel part is the only portion that requires additional components.

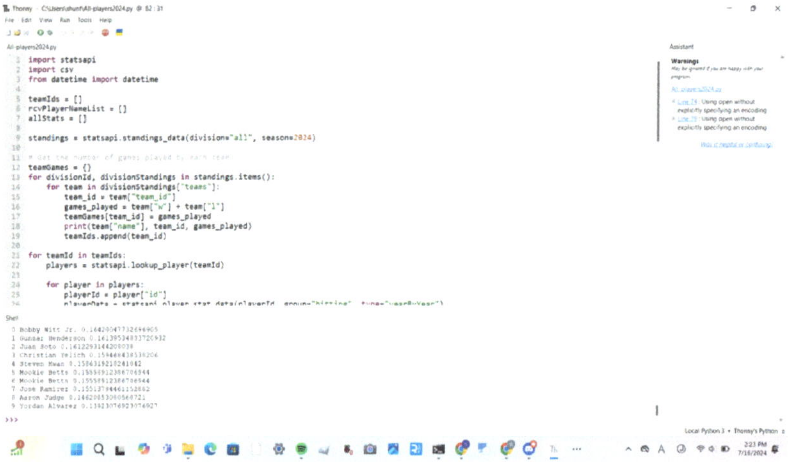

Fig. 1: Thonny Layout

There are various codes that you can run, depending on what you want to display. First, you can run `All-MLB2024.py`, which collects all qualified batters' basic hitting stats, calculates each of their RCVs, and records all the data in a chart.

Secondly, `All-Players2024.py` orders all qualified hitters of MLB from the best to the worst in terms of RCV. Next, you can run `Histogram.py`, which displays a histogram based on the chart made from `All-Players2024.py`. The histogram visualizes the trend throughout the whole league. If you run `Boxplot.py`, it creates a boxplot based on the data acquired from `All-Players2024.py`, the same data as the histogram.

Finally, the LED Panel part requires more components to be used, which will be explained later. The panel displays the top three and the bottom three every day, so you can see the updates in the leaderboard on a daily basis.

4.3.1 RCV charts

`All-Players2024.py` creates two types of charts. The program fetches the basic hitting stats of all qualified batters and calculates each of their RCVs. (A qualified batter must have 3.1 plate appearances (PA) per team game.) Then, it records all the data into a chart and saves the chart as `Allplayers.csv` (Fig. 2).

In `Allplayers.csv`, players are ordered based on their teams, from the teams of AL East, AL Central, AL West, NL East, NL Central, to NL West. This chart enables you to observe players' RCV in relation to their basic stats. You can also see how individual players perform compared to the team. There is a filtering tool that enables you to select the range of the RCV, apply criteria, etc.

The RCV is calculated with the following formula:

$$RCV = (1B \times 0.4 + 2B \times 0.7 + 3B \times 1.1 + HR \times 1.5 + (BB+HBP) \times 0.3 + SB \times 0.2 - SO \times 0.3 - CS \times 0.3 - GDP \times 1.3) / (PA-SF-SH)$$

	Name	singles	doubles	triples	HR	BB	HBP	SB	SO	CS	GDP	PA	SF	SH	RCV
1	Name	singles	doubles	triples	HR	BB	HBP	SB	SO	CS	GDP	PA	SF	SH	RCV
3	Gunnar He	57	18	5	28	47	6	14	102	1	1	432	2	0	0.286
5	Ryan Mou	57	22	1	12	21	1	3	77	0	11	366	4	0	0.271
7	Adley Ruts	72	12	0	16	36	1	1	70	0	6	404	4	0	0.275
9	Anthony S:	40	16	2	24	27	6	0	72	0	3	382	3	0	0.237
11	Jordan We	51	22	5	15	18	6	6	82	3	3	369	1	1	0.271
13	Aaron Jud|	46	24	1	34	72	6	5	106	0	14	424	2	0	0.306
15	Juan Soto	60	15	3	23	79	2	5	70	2	6	427	4	0	0.295
17	Gleyber To	54	15	0	8	36	3	4	86	3	5	380	5	2	0.231
19	Alex Verdu	54	19	1	10	30	1	1	60	1	9	394	6	0	0.235

Fig. 2: Allplayers.csv Chart (Partial)

By skimming through all the statistics that are involved in RCV, it is possible to see if there is any particular stat that influences the RCVs more than others. You can also learn what types of combinations of stats lead to certain RCV values.

`All-Players2024.py` creates another chart, `RCV.csv`, which is a simplified version of `Allplayers.csv` (Fig. 3). Instead of displaying all the basic stats of the players, it only contains the players' names and their respective RCV values.

	A	B	C
14			
15	0.153271	José Ramírez	
16			
17	0.147216	Aaron Judge	
18			
19	0.144203	Yordan Alvarez	
20			
21	0.141032	Anthony Santander	
22			
23	0.138928	Ketel Marte	
24			
25	0.137419	Jarren Duran	
26			
27	0.137365	Francisco Lindor	

Fig. 3: RCV.csv (Partial)

In `RCV.csv`, players are sorted based on their RCV values, from the player with the highest RCV to the one with the lowest RCV. This is essentially a leaderboard of RCV. You can use the "Find" tool in order to look for particular players and see what rank they are in. Furthermore, you can predict the top players and the bottom players and see if they match with reality. Unlike `Allplayers.csv`, it is easy to find players who excel in terms of RCV since it is already sorted.

4.3.2 RCV Histogram

The histogram is created based on the data of the whole league. It creates the ranges for each bar and their sizes fluctuate based on the frequency of the ranges (Fig. 4). The ranges gradually become smaller as the number of the bars increases, and vice versa. The range of each bar is defaulted as 0.1, but you can change it as you prefer by modifying the code.

With the histogram, you can quickly identify the distribution patterns within the graph. The code also gives lots of valuable information regarding the Histogram (Fig. 4). By combining either `All-Players2024.py` or `All-MLB2024.py` with `Histogram.py` to determine how well certain individuals are hitting in comparison to the rest of the league. It also gives other crucial information about the league.

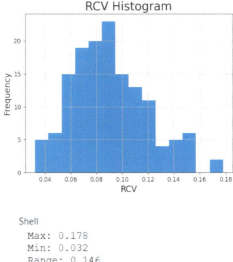

```
Shell
    Max: 0.178
    Min: 0.032
    Range: 0.146
    Mean: 0.09|
    Median: 0.088
    Mode: 0.089
    Mode-mean: 0.0014886718961900636
```

Fig. 4 RCV Histogram and its Statistical Properties

4.3.3 RCV Boxplot

Similar to the histogram, the boxplot that this code creates is based on the RCV of the whole league (Fig. 5). The boxplot divides the dataset into four quadrants, along with the outliers. It contains a box in the middle that indicates the interquartile range (IQR). The IQR range is from the 25th percentile of the whole data to the 75th percentile of the data. If a certain data point is within the IQR range, it is in the middle 50% of the data.

Unlike other visualization methods, the boxplot also contains outliers, which are data values outside the box by at least 1.5 times the IQR range. The outliers are helpful since they are generally representative of either the exceptional players or the complete opposite. Additionally, the whiskers represent the top 25% and the bottom 25%. Users can interpret these data values as players with high and low values.

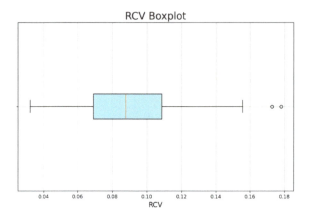

```
Shell
  complete row: []
  Max: 0.178
  Min: 0.032
  Range: 0.146
  Mean: 0.09
  Median: 0.088
  Q1: 0.069
  Q2: 0.088
  Q3: 0.108
  IQR: 0.039
  rightWhisker: 0.168
  leftWhisker: 0.01
```

Fig. 5 RCV Boxplot and its Statistical Properties

Fig. 6: RCV LED Panel

4.3.4 RCV LED Panel

RCV LED Panel shows the top three and the bottom three players with the highest RCV values and the lowest RCV values with a 64-pixel by 128-pixel LED panel (Fig. 6). It is attached to, and controlled by, a Raspberry Pi computer that runs Python code to calculate the RCV value of each player and update the displayed information periodically. Top and bottom players are displayed with different colors, so you can easily distinguish them. For running the RCV LED Panel, you need to follow the instructions in Section 4 and run the code in Section 5.

4.4 Use Cases

RCV Visualizer is suitable for anyone who is interested in sabermetrics. It may be used by anyone who is looking to find outstanding players or even horrible players.

For example, team managers can utilize the RCV Visualizer to find the players to acquire in the future. Other users can use it to easily analyze the data and use it for various purposes such as betting. With these features, you can see it at a glance without having to calculate everything manually. This is useful when you want to compare the RCV of all players across the league. It is easy to understand even for beginners because it is expressed in visually clear methods.

Here's a potential use case. Let's say you are in a fantasy baseball league with your friends. The winner receives $100 from everyone else. You are very desperate for the prize. You use the RCV Visualizer and find out that a player named "Joe Random" has recorded phenomenal RCV performance, and you believe that he has the potential to become a star player. Two months pass by, and you are in first place in the fantasy league. Then, you realize that "Joe Random" was the best performer on your team, single-handedly carrying you all the way to first place.

Furthermore, Instead of displaying the players who are performing well, it is also possible to display the players who are performing badly. This way, you would know to avoid these players.

4.5 Hardware Setup

This section explains how to build the RCV LED Panel. Here is a list of required parts:

- Raspberry Pi (1x): Out of the many types of Raspberry Pi models, I used Raspberry Pi 3 Model A+. It does not come with a power supply cable and a MicroSD card. You need to purchase them too.

- LED matrix boards (2x): Use two 64x64 RGB LED matrix boards. Amazon Standard Identification Number (ASIN): B0B3F7WKJ1. It includes a ribbon cable (x2), a screw terminal block (1x) and a power cable (1x).

- Male to male jumper wires (1-20x): ASIN: B089FZ79CS

- Adapter for LED matrix boards (1x): This board simplifies the wiring of up to three LED boards with a Raspberry Pi [1]. It is stacked onto a Raspberry Pi's 40-pin GPIO header (Fig. 7) to connect ribbon cables to LED boards.

ASINs can be used for product searches at `https://www.amazon.com`.

Fig. 7: Raspberry Pi 3 A+

4.5.1 Connecting the Panel-to-Raspi adapter to the Raspi

With your Raspberry Pi turned off, stack the Raspi-to-panel adapter on the Raspberry Pi's 40-pin GPIO header (Fig. 7). Make sure that the adapter is right on top of the Raspi, and not tilted.

4.5.2 Connecting the adapter to the LED Panel

Next, connect the gray ribbon cable to the Raspi-to-Panel adapter. Find the three black connectors on the adapter. Plug the gray ribbon cable into the bottom left one. (Fig. 8).

Fig 8: Gray Ribbon Cable connected to the Adapter

5.3 Connecting the first LED Panels to the adapter

Flip one of your LED Panels to see the backside. Make sure to rotate the panel properly, so the directions of the four arrows match with the image (Fig. 9). The top and the bottom arrows should be pointing upwards, and the two middle row arrows should be pointing upwards, and the two middle row arrows should be pointing to the right.

There are two connectors on the panel. One of them should be labeled "JIN", "IN", or something else similar. This one is the input connector. The other should be labeled "JOUT", "OUT", or something else similar. This one is the output connector. Connect the gray ribbon cable on the adapter to the input connector (Fig. 10).

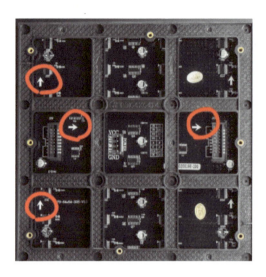

Fig. 9: Backside of an LED Panel

Fig. 10: Adapter connected to an LED Panel

Finally, find a box of 2 x 4 holes on the Raspi-to-Panel adapter. Then, find the #E and the #P8 holes from the box. Connect them with a jumper wire.

5.4 Connecting the Power Cable

Connect the two parts of the power supply cable. Connect one end to a power outlet and insert the other to a screw terminal block (Fig. 11).

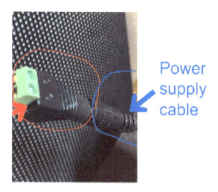

Fig. 11: Power Supply Cable Connection

Next, have a black and red power cable ready. There are two wires of the power cable that have metal ends. Insert the one with the red wire into the "+" hole of the screw terminal block, and insert the black wire one to the "−" hole of the screw terminal block (Fig. 12).

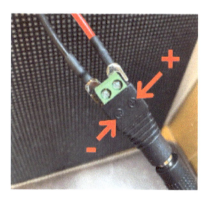

Fig. 12 Black and Red Power Cables

After that, connect one of the power cable's plastic ends to the power connector of the LED Panel, which is located in the center of the panel.

4.5.5 Connecting the second LED Panel

Have another gray ribbon cable and LED Panel ready. Place the second panel side by side with the panel that is already connected. The second panel should be on the right side. The directions of the arrows on the second panel should be exactly the same as those of the first panel. Now insert one end of the gray ribbon cable to the output connector of the first panel. Then, insert the other end to the input connector of the second panel. Finally, connect the second plastic end of the power cable to the power connector of the second panel. The final setup should look something like this (Fig. 13).

Fig. 13: Completed Setup

4.6 Coding

This section explains the code for the RCV Visualizer. You can alter the colored parts according to your preferences.

4.6.1 All-Players.py

This section shows **All-Players.py**. See Section 4.3 for the functionalities of this code. It uses the MLB-StatsAPI module (**statsapi**) to download MLB stats data [2]. The module is a Python wrapper for MLB's Stats API [3]. It allows your code to access MLB's Stats API and obtain stats data as textual (string) data or Python objects such as lists and dictionaries [2, 4].

```
import statsapi, csv
from datetime import datetime

teamIds = []
rcvPlayerNameList = []
```

```
allStats = []

standings = statsapi.standings_data(division="all", season=2024)

teamGames = {}
for divisionId, divisionStandings in standings.items():
    for team in divisionStandings["teams"]:
        team_id = team["team_id"]
        games_played = team["w"] + team["l"]
        teamGames[team_id] = games_played
        print(team["name"], team_id, games_played)
        teamIds.append(team_id)

for teamId in teamIds:
    players = statsapi.lookup_player(teamId)

    for player in players:
        playerId = player["id"]
        playerData = statsapi.player_stat_data(
                             playerId,
                             group="hitting",
                             type="yearByYear")
        stats = playerData["stats"]
        playerPitchingData = statsapi.player_stat_data(
                             playerId,
                             group="pitching",
                             type="yearByYear")
        if playerPitchingData["stats"]:
            continue

        if len(stats) != 0:
            print(player["fullName"], playerId)
            mostRecentSeasonStats = stats[-1]
            hittingStats = mostRecentSeasonStats["stats"]
        else:
            continue

        PA = hittingStats.get("plateAppearances", 0)

        if PA / teamGames[teamId] < 3.1:
            continue

        doubles = hittingStats.get("doubles", 0)
        triples = hittingStats.get("triples", 0)
        HR      = hittingStats.get("homeRuns", 0)
        singles = hittingStats.get("hits", 0) - doubles - triples - HR
        BB      = hittingStats.get("baseOnBalls", 0)
        HBP     = hittingStats.get("hitByPitch", 0)
        SB      = hittingStats.get("stolenBases", 0)
        SO      = hittingStats.get("strikeOuts", 0)
        CS      = hittingStats.get("caughtStealing", 0)
        GDP     = hittingStats.get("groundIntoDoublePlay", 0)
        SF      = hittingStats.get("sacFlies", 0)
        SH      = hittingStats.get("sacBunts", 0)
        Div     = PA - SF - SH

        if Div != 0:
            RCV = (singles * 0.4 + doubles * 0.7 + triples * 1.1 +
                   HR * 1.5 + BB * 0.3 + HBP * 0.3 + SB * 0.2 -
                   SO * 0.3 - CS * 0.3 - GDP * 1.3) / Div
            print("RCV:", RCV)
```

```
            rcvPlayerNameList.append([RCV, player["fullName"]])
            allStats.append([player["fullName"], singles, doubles,
                             triples, HR, BB, HBP, SB, SO, CS, GDP,
                             PA, SF, SH, RCV])

sortedRcvPlayerNameList = sorted(rcvPlayerNameList, reverse=True)

dt = datetime.now().isoformat()
today = dt.split("T")[0]

with open("rcv-" + today + ".csv", 'w') as f:
    writer = csv.writer(f)
    writer.writerow(["RCV", "Name"])
    writer.writerows(sortedRcvPlayerNameList)

with open("allplayers-" + today + ".csv", 'w') as f:
    writer = csv.writer(f)
    writer.writerow(["Name", "singles", "doubles", "triples", "HR",
                     "BB", "HBP", "SB", "SO", "CS", "GDP", "PA",
                     "SF", "SH", "RCV"])
    writer.writerows(allStats)
```

4.6.2 Histogram.py

This section shows `Histogram.py`. See Section 4.3.2 for the function-alities of this code. It uses the Matplotlib module (`matplotlib`) to draw a histogram [5].

```
import csv, statistics, matplotlib.pyplot as plt
from datetime import datetime

rcvPlayerNameList = []
rcvList = []

dt = datetime.now().isoformat()
today = dt.split("T")[0]

with open("rcv-" + today + ".csv", "r") as f:
    reader = csv.reader(f)
    next(reader)
    for row in reader:
        if len(row) < 2:
            print(f"complete row: {row}")
            continue
        try:
            rcvPlayerNameList.append([float(row[0]), row[1]])
            rcvList.append(float(row[0]))
        except ValueError as ve:
            print(f"Skipping row with invalid data: {row} ({ve})")

rcvMax =    rcvList[0]
rcvMin =    rcvList[-1]
rcvRange =  rcvList[0] - rcvList[-1]
rcvMean =   statistics.mean(rcvList)
rcvMedian = statistics.median(rcvList)

print("Max:", round(rcvMax, 3))
```

56

```
print("Min:",    round(rcvMin, 3))
print("Range:",  round(rcvRange, 3))
print("Mean:",   round(rcvMean, 3))
print("Median:", round(rcvMedian, 3))

plt.title("RCV Histogram", fontsize=20)
plt.xlabel("RCV",          fontsize=14)
plt.ylabel("Frequency",    fontsize=14)
plt.grid(True)

freqs, bins, patches = plt.hist(rcvList,
                                bins=int(rcvRange/0.01))
modeIndex = freqs.argmax()
rcvMode = round((bins[modeIndex] + bins[modeIndex+1])/2, 3)

print("Mode:",        rcvMode)
print("Mode-mean:",   abs(rcvMode - rcvMean))
print("Median-mean:", abs(rcvMedian - rcvMean))

plt.show()
```

4.6.3 Boxplot.py

This section shows `Boxplot.py`. See Section 4.3.3 for the functionalities of this code. It uses the Matplotlib module (`matplotlib`) to draw a boxplot [5]. The `statistics` and `numpy` modules are used to calculate mean, median and percentile values.

```
import csv, statistics, matplotlib.pyplot as plt, numpy as np
from datetime import datetime

rcvPlayerNameList = []
rcvList = []

dt = datetime.now().isoformat()
today = dt.split("T")[0]

with open("rcv-" + today + ".csv", "r") as f:
    reader = csv.reader(f)
    next(reader)
    for row in reader:
        if len(row) < 2:
            print(f"complete row: {row}")
            continue
        try:
            rcvPlayerNameList.append([float(row[0]), row[1]])
            rcvList.append(float(row[0]))
        except ValueError as ve:
            print(f"Skipping row with invalid data: {row} ({ve})")

rcvMax =    max(rcvList)
rcvMin =    min(rcvList)
rcvRange =  rcvMax - rcvMin
rcvMean =   statistics.mean(rcvList)
rcvMedian = statistics.median(rcvList)
q1, q2, q3 = np.percentile(rcvList, [25, 50, 75])
iqr = q3 - q1
```

```
rightWhisker = q3 + 1.5 * iqr
leftWhisker =  q1 - 1.5 * iqr

print("Max:",        round(rcvMax, 3))
print("Min:",        round(rcvMin, 3))
print("Range:",      round(rcvRange, 3))
print("Mean:",       round(rcvMean, 3))
print("Median:",     round(rcvMedian, 3))
print("Q1:",         round(q1, 3))
print("Q2:",         round(q2, 3))
print("Q3:",         round(q3, 3))
print("IQR:",        round(iqr, 3))
print("rightWhisker:", round(rightWhisker, 3))
print("leftWhisker:",  round(leftWhisker, 3))

plt.figure(figsize=(10, 6))
plt.boxplot(rcvList, vert=False, patch_artist=True,
            boxprops=dict(facecolor="lightblue"))

plt.title("RCV Boxplot", fontsize=20)
plt.xlabel("RCV",        fontsize=14)
plt.grid(True)

plt.show()
```

4.6.4 LEDPanel.py

This section shows **LEDPanel.py**. See Section 4.3.4 for the functionalities of this code. It uses the **rgbmatrix** module to display stats data on LED matrix boards [6]. The Pillow module (**PIL**) is used to generate an image to be displayed on LED matrix boards. The size of each image is 128-pixel by 64-pixel landscape because the RCV Visualizer uses two LED matrix boards side by side (Fig. 6).

```
import statsapi, csv, time
from datetime import datetime
from rgbmatrix import RGBMatrix, RGBMatrixOptions
from PIL import Image, ImageDraw, ImageFont

def calculate_rcv(hittingStats):
    doubles = hittingStats.get("doubles", 0)
    triples = hittingStats.get("triples", 0)
    HR =      hittingStats.get("homeRuns", 0)
    singles = hittingStats.get("hits", 0) - doubles - triples - HR
    BB =      hittingStats.get("baseOnBalls", 0)
    HBP =     hittingStats.get("hitByPitch", 0)
    SB =      hittingStats.get("stolenBases", 0)
    SO =      hittingStats.get("strikeOuts", 0)
    CS =      hittingStats.get("caughtStealing", 0)
    GDP =     hittingStats.get("groundIntoDoublePlay", 0)
    PA =      hittingStats.get("plateAppearances", 0)
    SF =      hittingStats.get("sacFlies", 0)
    SH =      hittingStats.get("sacBunts", 0)
    Div =     PA - SF - SH
    if Div != 0:
```

```
            return (singles * 0.4 + doubles * 0.7 + triples * 1.1 +
                    HR * 1.5 + BB * 0.3 + HBP * 0.3 + SB * 0.2 -
                    SO * 0.3 - CS * 0.3 - GDP * 1.3) / Div
        else:
            return 0

options = RGBMatrixOptions()
options.cols = 128
options.rows = 64
options.parallel = 1
options.gpio_slowdown = 3
options.drop_privileges = False

rcvPlayerNameList = []
allStats = []

standings = statsapi.standings_data(division="all", season=2024)
teamGames = {}
for divisionId, divisionStandings in standings.items():
    for team in divisionStandings["teams"]:
        team_id = team["team_id"]
        games_played = team["w"] + team["l"]
        teamGames[team_id] = games_played

for teamId in teamGames.keys():
    players = statsapi.lookup_player(teamId)
    for player in players:
        playerId = player["id"]
        playerData = statsapi.player_stat_data(
                        playerId,
                        group="hitting",
                        type="yearByYear")
        stats = playerData["stats"]
        playerPitchingData = statsapi.player_stat_data(
                                playerId,
                                group="pitching",
                                type="yearByYear")
        if playerPitchingData["stats"]:
            continue

        if len(stats) != 0:
            mostRecentSeasonStats = stats[-1]
            hittingStats = mostRecentSeasonStats["stats"]
        else:
            continue

        PA = hittingStats.get("plateAppearances", 0)
        if PA / teamGames[teamId] < 3.1:
            continue

        RCV = calculate_rcv(hittingStats)
        rcvPlayerNameList.append([RCV, player["fullName"]])
        allStats.append([player["fullName"], RCV])

sortedRcvPlayerNameList = sorted(rcvPlayerNameList,
                                 key=lambda x: x[0], reverse=True)

dt = datetime.now().isoformat()
today = dt.split("T")[0]

with open("rcv-" + today + ".csv", 'w') as f:
```

```
        writer = csv.writer(f)
        writer.writerow(["RCV", "Name"])
        writer.writerows(sortedRcvPlayerNameList)

with open("allplayers-" + today + ".csv", 'w') as f:
        writer = csv.writer(f)
        writer.writerow(["Name", "RCV"])
        writer.writerows(allStats)

imageWidth = 128
imageHeight = 64
image = Image.new("RGB", (imageWidth, imageHeight), (0, 0, 0))
draw = ImageDraw.Draw(image)
font = ImageFont.load_default()

for i in range(min(3, len(sortedRcvPlayerNameList))):
        player = sortedRcvPlayerNameList[i]
        draw.text((0, i * 8),
                    player[1],
                    fill=(255, 255, 0),
                    font=font)
        draw.text((100, i * 8),
                    f"{player[0]:.3f}",
                    fill=(255, 255, 0),
                    font=font)

for i in range(min(3, len(sortedRcvPlayerNameList))):
        player = sortedRcvPlayerNameList[-(i+1)]
        draw.text((0, (i + 3) * 8),
                    player[1],
                    fill=(255, 255, 255),
                    font=font)
        draw.text((100, (i + 3) * 8),
                    f"{player[0]:.3f}",
                    fill=(255, 255, 255),
                    font=font)

matrix = RGBMatrix(options=options)
matrix.SetImage(image)

try:
        while True:
            time.sleep(100)
except KeyboardInterrupt:
        sys.exit(0)
```

This code runs an infinite loop in the end, so it can keep displaying RCV data (the top three and bottom three players with the highest RCV and lowest RCV values) on LED matrix boards. To stop running this code, hit the Control (Ctrl) and C keys on your keyboard.

You can edit the parts that have blue fonts based on your preference. For instance, you can change the standards for determining the outliers. Additionally, "fill=(x,y,z)" indicates a color in terms of RGB, which fills certain components of the graph.

Once you are done customizing, congratulations! You have completed the RCV Visualizer. Run the code and test out the system to see if it works as you expect.

4.7. Future Steps

There are a few ways that my project can be improved. One way is to make a program that automatically finds which players are the most valuable and which ones are the least valuable. By taking into account the data of the whole league, it is possible to evaluate each player properly in comparison to other players. Another step is to code in order to make this process automatic.

I would also like to perform the same actions for pitchers' stat categories instead of batters'. Similar to the batters' stat categories, Making a stat category for pitchers on my own would also be a logical future step as well.

4.8 Conclusion

I was looking forward to PhysTech 2024 since I was interested in creating projects related to physical activities. Despite having an obscure idea of what kind of project to do, I was unsure of how to make the project user-friendly.

Although there are not a lot of physical building components to the project, RCV Visualizer consists of various intricate codes, each serving their own purpose. Therefore, it is crucial to be organized and careful with the different codes. Additionally, because there are many ways to display the data, it is necessary to logically determine which method is optimal. For instance, if you want to know the range of the most common RCV values, the histogram is the best choice.

I struggled with writing the codes that function smoothly without any errors. The histogram part was especially difficult since the code was very different from All-MLB 204.py and All-Players 2024.py. Thus, I encountered a lot of errors, which required constant debugging. In case you also need to perform some debugging, remember to stay calm and not panic.

Despite a number of challenges, I managed to complete this project. I hope you will find success and enjoyment in accomplishing this project!

References

[1] https://www.electrodragon.com/product/rgb-matrix-panel-drive-board-raspberry-pi/

[2] https://github.com/toddrob99/MLB-StatsAPI

[3] https://statsapi.mlb.com/

[4] Nathan Braun, Learn to Code with Baseball, https://codebaseball.com/

[5] https://matplotlib.org/

[6] https://github.com/hzeller/rpi-rgb-led-matrix

[7] https://github.com/python-pillow/Pillow

Biography

Shun Nagata is a sports enthusiast who loves data analytics and coding. He co-founded PhysTech and co-chaired its inaugural edition in 2024. Currently a 11th grader, Shun is a starting center-midfielder in the varsity soccer team while playing on a club team. He has won a few league/tournament championships, such as a championship in the local high school league consisting of around 8 schools. He is also a JV baseball player. Shun has a strong interest in data analytics, especially sabermetrics. He studies various baseball stats and practices them in fantasy baseball leagues. He even developed a new stat category of his own and has been analyzing it with real game datasets. Shun exercises his Python coding skill to implement the baseball stats and build Internet of Things devices. In order to improve his programming skills, he took the PCEP exam and received the PCEP certificate. Shun has been volunteering in many ways for various communities, such as teaching others about the Internet of Things devices. His service was awarded by the president of the U.S. and he received the President's Volunteer Service Award. He won the Silver Prize at AnimalHack 2023.

Chapter 5

Portable WBGT Tracker for Outdoor Athletes in the Heat

Hanna Suzuki

Bedford High School
Bedford, MA 01730, USA

Abstract

WBGT Tracker is a portable device that can find and display the local Web Bulb Globe Temperature (WBGT), which indicates heat stress on the human body in direct sunlight. This device allows outdoor athletes to be aware of the environmental conditions for their activities and warn them early to take precautions. It is built with a Raspberry Pi computer to run Python code that downloads WBGT forecasts from the National Oceanic and Atmospheric Administration (NOAA) and shows them on an e-paper display.

5.1 Introduction

Heat-related illnesses are a critical threat for outdoor athletes in the summer months. They impact athletes' conditions, performance, careers and even lives. At the 2021 Tokyo Olympics, which was the hottest Olympic Games on record with temperatures of 93°F (34°C) and humidity of 70%, Tennis player Daniil Medvedev (the Games' number two seed) spoke of "dying on court" during the heat of a match [1]. In the Rings of Fire report, published by the British Association for Sustainable Sport, Olympic bronze medal tennis player Marcus Daniell describes the heat as "true risk – the type of risk that could potentially be fatal" [2].

This project builds a portable device, called WBGT Tracker, which can find and display the Web Bulb Globe Temperature (WBGT) at an area of athletic activity. WBGT is a numerical indicator of heat stress on the human body in direct sunlight. WBGT Tracker allows athletes to be aware of the environmental conditions for their activities and warn them early to take precautions, for example taking breaks frequently in the shade and keeping hydrated.

WBGT Tracker is implemented with a small (credit-card sized) computer called Raspberry Pi. A Python program runs on Raspberry Pi to determine the current location of the device (latitude and longitude) through IP geolocation and download WBGT forecast for that location from the National Oceanic and Atmospheric Administration (NOAA). It shows the forecast and heat safety alert on an e-paper display. WBGT tracker can be activated via iOS Siri.

Figs. 1 and 2 show how WBGT Tracker looks like. Since it uses an e-paper display, it can hold the information displayed even if it is turned off. It can be activated at home, in a car, or at a clubhouse, and then brought to a practice or a match without a power source.

Fig. 1: WBGT Tracker attached to a Tennis Bag (1)

Fig. 2: WBGT Tracker attached to a Tennis Bag (2)

5.2 Background

This section overviews heat-related illnesses, describes Wet Bulb Globe Temperature (WBGT), and summarizes WBGT-based heat safety policies for high school athletes.

5.2.1 Heat-related Illnesses

Heat-related illnesses such as heat cramps, heat exhaustion and heat stroke should be taken into concern when doing sports and other outdoor activities in the summer months. Heat stroke is the most serious heat-related illness and a top cause of preventable death for high school athletes [3, 4, 5]. Symptoms of heat stroke include high body temperature, sweating profusely, dizziness, confusion, headache, losing consciousness, and seizures.

Heat stroke occurs when the body is too overheating to regulate its temperature. High air temperature and direct sunlight exposure increase body temperature. Exercise (muscle contraction) also causes an increase in body temperature. During intense exercise, heat production is 15 to 20 times greater than at rest and can raise body core temperature 1°C (1.8°F) every 5 minutes unless heat is removed [6].

The body strives to regulate its temperature by releasing heat from the skin via evaporation of sweat. Wind accelerates the loss of heat. However, when dehydrated, the sweating mechanism does not work properly. It is also impaired as humidity increases. No extra heat loss can be expected when there is no wind. Due to these factors, the body fails to cool down and cause heat stroke. When heat stroke occurs, the body temperature can rise to 105°F (40.5°C) or higher in 10 to 15 minutes [7].

5.2.2 Wet Bulb Globe Temperature (WBGT)

Wet Bulb Globe Temperature (WBGT) is the most effective method to estimate the threat of heat-related illness. It integrates the influences of sun exposure, air temperature, humidity and wind movement. It is an "apparent temperature," or "feels-like temperature," which indicates the human perception of temperature.

WBGT is measured with three different thermometers: dry-bulb, wet-bulb and black-globe thermometers [8]. A dry-bulb thermometer measures the actual air temperature. A wet-bulb thermometer is a thermometer wrapped in a water-moisturized cloth. It behaves differently from a dry-bulb thermometer by taking humidity and wind into account. The less humid the air is, the faster the water will evaporate. The faster water evaporates, the lower the thermometer's temperature will be relative to air temperature. A black globe thermometer is a thermometer inside a black globe. The black surface absorbs solar heat, and the surface temperature is affected by wind.

WBGT is calculated as a weighted mean of the data inputs from these thermometers: dry-bulb temperature (T_d), wet-bulb temperature (T_w) and black-globe temperature (T_g):

$$WBGT = 0.7 * T_w + 0.2 * T_g + 0.1 * T_d$$

If T_d, T_w and T_g are measured in Fahrenheit (F), WBGT is computed in F. If they are in Celsius (C), WBGT is computed in C.

As this equation shows, WBGT places a very high weight for wet-bulb temperature (T_w), compared to dry-bulb temperature (T_d), because it is intended to emphasize the large impact humidity has on the body's ability to sweat and release heat. Although many people look at air temperature and determine the safety of being active outside, this can be misleading. Even when air temperature is on the lower side, it can still be dangerous if humidity is extremely high and there is no wind. WBGT can quantify this risk effectively.

WBGT is similar to the heat index because both are apparent temperatures calculated with air temperature and humidity. However, the heat index uses air temperature in the shade. This is not a reasonable assumption for outdoor athletes. In contrast, WBGT places a higher weight for black-globe temperature (T_g) than dry-bulb temperature (T_d) to emphasize the impacts of direct sunlight on body temperature.

As a result, professional, national, and state athletic associations have accepted WBGT as the primary means of determining the appropriate temperatures for hot weather activities. For example, the United States Tennis Association sets WBGT-based heat policies for junior singles, wheelchair singles, women's open singles and men's open singles matches in the US Open Championships [9]. The United States Soccer Federation's player health and safety program, called Recognize to Recover, provides WBGT-based heat safety guidelines [10].

5.2.3 WBGT-based Heat Policies for High School Athletes

The National Athletic Trainers' Association (NATA), which organizes the largest community of high school athletic trainers in the US, released a position statement about heat-related illnesses in 2015 [11]. It uses WBGT as a means of measuring environmental risk factors and offers an example WBGT-based safety policy. It also points out that a "one size fits all" heat policy does not work across different geographical regions in the US.

By analyzing regional variations in acclimatization to heat based on climatology research findings, Grundstein et al. define three regions in the US (Fig. 3) and propose a WBGT-based heat policy for each region (Fig. 4) [12]. As shown in Fig. 4, northern regions (Category 1) have lower WBGT thresholds for activity modification than other regions (Categories 2 and 3) because athletes in the North are less acclimatized to heat than in other regions.

CATEGORY 1
CATEGORY 2
CATEGORY 3

Fig. 3: Regional Categories based on Acclimatization to Heat. Determined with the 90th Percentile Warm Season Maximum Daily WBGT. Excerpt from [10].

ALERT LEVEL	WBGT BY REGION (°F)			EVENT CONDITIONS	RECOMMENDED WORK TO REST RATIOS (ACTIONS & BREAKS)
	CAT 1	CAT 2	CAT 3		
BLACK	>86.2°	>89.8°	>92.0°	Extreme Conditions	No Outdoor Training, delay training until cooler, or Cancel Training.
RED	84.2-86.1°	87.8-89.7°	90.1-91.9°	High Risk for Heat Related Illness	Maximum of 1 hour of training with 4 by 4 minute breaks within the hour. No additional conditioning allowed.
ORANGE	81.1-84.1°	84.7-87.7°	87.1-90.0°	Moderate Risk for Heat Related Illness	Maximum of 2 hours of training with 4 by 4 minute breaks each hour, OR a 10 minute break every 30 minutes of training.
YELLOW	76.3-81.0°	79.9-84.6°	82.2-87.0°	Less than Ideal Conditions	3 Separate 4 minute breaks each hour, OR a 12 minute break every 40 minutes of training
GREEN	<76.1°	<79.8°	<82.1°	Good Conditions	Normal Activities. 3 Separate 3 minute breaks each hour of training, OR a 10 minute break every 40 minutes

Fig. 4: WBGT Thresholds for Heat Alert Levels in each Regional Category. Excerpt from [10].

Currently, this is the most widely-used heat policy for high school athletes. It is recommended by the National Federation of State High School Associations (NFHS), which writes the rules of competition for most high school sports and activities in the US [13, 14]. Most high schools in the US (more than 18,000 high schools) belong to NFHS through their state's high school associations. For example, the Massachusetts Interscholastic Athletic Association (MIAA) is a member of NFHS, and it consists of more than 370 high schools in Massachusetts. Following NFHS' recommendation, MIAA sponsors activities and competitions in 33 sports based on the Category 1 WBGT thresholds in [12] [15, 16].

In this project, WBGT Tracker downloads the local WBGT forecast from NOAA and identifies one of five alert levels based on the forecast and regional category.

5.3 Hardware Setup

WBGT Tracker is built with a Raspberry Pi and an e-paper display.

- Raspberry Pi Zero 2 WH (1x): Purchase a MicroSD card separately. It does not come with a Raspberry Pi. Amazon Standard Identification Number (ASIN): B09LTDQY2Z. This project uses the Version 2 of Raspberry Pi Zero (Zero 2 WH), but its Version 1 works too (Zero WH; ASIN: B0CG99MR5W).

- Pimoroni Inky pHAT (1x): This is a 2.13" e-paper display that can use black, white and red colors. It has 2x20 GPIO sockets (holes); it can sit directly on top of Raspberry Pi's GPIO header. Its display dimension (48.5mm width x 23.8mm height) perfectly fits with the footprint of Raspberry Pi Zero. This display is designed to be clearly visible even in bright sunlight. Adafruit Product ID: 3743. Pimoroni's product Web page: [17].

- Flirc Aluminum Case for Raspberry Pi Zero (1x): It is highly recommended to place a Raspberry Pi in a case because WBGT Tracker is intended to be a portable device that is attached to a sports bag and used outdoors. ASIN: B08837L144. Adafruit product ID: 4822.

ASINs can be used for product searches at `https://www.amazon.com`, and Adafruit product IDs can be used at `https://www.adafruit.com`.

Fig. 5 shows how WBGT Tracker is assembled with the required components.

Fig. 5: Fully assembled WBGT Tracker

5.4 Software Setup

WBGT Tracker runs Python code in Raspberry Pi to determine the current location of the device (latitude and longitude) through IP geolocation and download WBGT forecast for that location from the National Digital Forecast Database (NDFD). NDFD is developed by the National Oceanic and Atmospheric Administration (NOAA) for the National Weather Service [18]. Then, the Python code displays the downloaded forecast and heat safety alert. This section describes how to set up and run the Python code with the Inky.

5.4.1 Setting up an Inky pHAT

First, turn on the Raspberry Pi and update its operating system by running the following commands one by one on a Terminal.

- `sudo apt update -y`
- `sudo apt full-upgrade -y`

Then, enable I2C and SPI communication with the Raspberry Pi Configuration settings. To install a driver for the Inky pHAT e-display, run the following command on a Terminal.

- `curl https://get.pimoroni.com/inky | bash`

See [19] for the reference manual of Inky pHAT.

5.4.2 Setting up the Required Python Modules

NDFD provides a REST API that returns XML data in the Digital Weather Markup Language (DWML). To convert the downloaded XML data to a Python dictionary, you need the **xmltodict** module. Install it by running the following command on a Terminal:

- `sudo pip3 install xmltodict`

The next step is to download **noaa_wbgt.py** from the **code** folder at [20] and run it to confirm REST API access to NDFD. Data downloading is successful if you see an output that contains WBGT data.

WBGT Tracker also requires the **geocoder** module, which implements IP geolocation [20]. This feature locates a geographical area where an IP address is used and returns the latitude and longitude of the area's center. Install the module by running the following command on a Terminal:

- `sudo pip3 install geocoder`

Run the following code to test IP geolocation:

```
import geocoder
geoInfo = geocoder.ip("me")
lat = geoInfo.lat
lon = geoInfo.lng
print(lat, lon)
```

5.4.3 Python Code

WBGT Tracker runs the following Python code, which is available as **wbgt.py** in the **code** folder at [21]. Make sure to place this code and **noaa_wbgt.py** in the same folder.

```
import geocoder
from noaa_wbgt import getWbgt
from inky import InkyPHAT
from PIL import Image, ImageFont, ImageDraw
```

```python
regionCategory = 1

fontBig =       ImageFont.truetype("JetBrainsMono-Regular.ttf", 35)
fontSmall =     ImageFont.truetype("JetBrainsMono-Regular.ttf", 25)
fontSmaller = ImageFont.truetype("JetBrainsMono-Regular.ttf", 20)


def getLatLon():
    geoInfo = geocoder.ip("me")
    return (geoInfo.lat, geoInfo.lng)

def getAlertCondition(wbgt, regionCategory):
    assert regionCategory in [1, 2, 3], "Invalid region number: " +\
           str(regionCategory) + "." + " It must be 1, 2 or 3."

    if regionCategory == 1:
        if   wbgt > 86.1: condition = "Extreme"
        elif wbgt > 84.1: condition = "High Risk"
        elif wbgt > 81.0: condition = "Moderate Risk"
        elif wbgt > 76.1: condition = "Less than Ideal"
        else:             condition = "Good conditions"
    elif regionCategory == 2:
        if   wbgt > 89.7: condition = "Extreme"
        elif wbgt > 87.7: condition = "High Risk"
        elif wbgt > 84.6: condition = "Moderate Risk"
        elif wbgt > 79.8: condition = "Less than Ideal"
        else:             condition = "Good conditions"
    elif regionCategory == 3:
        if   wbgt > 91.9: condition = "Extreme"
        elif wbgt > 90.0: condition = "High Risk"
        elif wbgt > 87.0: condition = "Moderate Risk"
        elif wbgt > 82.1: condition = "Less than Ideal"
        else:             condition = "Good conditions"
    return condition


def maxWbgtHrToHrDuration(maxWbgt):
    maxTime = []
    for key, value in timeToWbgtDictToday.items():
        if value == maxWbgt:
            maxTime.append(key)

    date = maxTime[0]
    shortDate = date[5:10]

    maxTimeHr = []
    for item in maxTime:
        Hr = int(item[11:13])
        if   Hr > 12: Hr = str(Hr - 12) + "PM"
        else:         Hr = str(Hr)      + "AM"
        maxTimeHr.append(Hr)

    maxTimeHrStr = ""
    if len(maxTimeHr) == 1:
        maxTimeHrStr = maxTimeHr[0]
    else:
        maxTimeHrStr = maxTimeHr[0] + " ~ " + maxTimeHr[-1]
    return (shortDate, maxTimeHrStr)
```

```
def displayWbgtInfo(date, maxWbgt, maxWbgtHrToHrDuration, alertCondi-
tion):
    display = InkyPHAT("red")
    image = Image.new("P", (display.WIDTH, display.HEIGHT),
                      display.WHITE)
    draw = ImageDraw.Draw(image)

    draw.text((0,0), "WBGT" + " " + date, display.BLACK,
              font=fontSmaller)
    draw.text((0, 25), str(maxWbgt) + "F ", display.RED,
              font=fontBig)
    draw.text((70, 30), maxWbgtHrToHrDuration, display.BLACK,
              font=fontSmall)
    draw.text((0, 70), alertCondition, display.RED,
              font=fontSmaller)
    display.set_image(image)
    display.show()



lat, lon = getLatLon()
currentWbgt, timeToWbgtDictToday, timeToWbgtDictTomorrow, time-
ToWbgtDictWeek = getWbgt(lat, lon)

maxWbgt = max(timeToWbgtDictToday.values())
todayDate, hrToHr = maxWbgtHrToHrDuration(maxWbgt)
alertCond = getAlertCondition(maxWbgt, regionCategory)

displayWbgtInfo(todayDate, maxWbgt, hrToHr, alertCond)
```

This code performs IP geolocation in the **getLatLon()** function to retrieve the latitude and longitude of an area where WBGT Tracker is used and passes them to the function **getWbgt()**. This function returns the current WBGT and WBGT forecasts (today's, tomorrow's and weekly forecasts) with NDFD.

The Python code extracts the highest WBGT from today's forecast and identifies the duration (from what time to what time) of the highest WBGT with the **maxWbgtHrToHrDuration()** function. Then, it determines the heat alert condition for the highest WBGT ("extreme," "high risk," "moderate risk," "less than ideal," or "good") according to a given regional category. The regional category is set in the **regionCategory** variable. Category 1 is used by default, but it can be changed to Categories 2 or 3.

In the end, the Python code calls the **displayWbgtInfo()** function to show all the collected data on the e-paper display (Fig. 5). It takes about 15 seconds to refresh the display. As mentioned earlier, the display can keep showing the data even after Raspberry Pi is turned off. You can bring WBGT Tracker to a practice or a match without a power source.

To clear the information displayed, run the following Python code, which is available as **clear.py** in the **code** folder at [20].

```
from inky import InkyPHAT
from PIL import Image, ImageFont, ImageDraw

display = InkyPHAT()
image = Image.new("P",
                  (display.WIDTH, display.HEIGHT),
                  display.BLACK)
display.set_image(image)
display.show()
```

5.5 Future Work

WBGT Tracker can be improved further in several ways. Currently, it uses WBGT forecasts from NOAA's NDFD and performs early safety warnings for athletes ahead of their practices or matches. The next step is to perform real-time safety warnings during a practice or match in addition to early warnings. On-site WBGT measurement is required to issue accurate real-time warnings. A challenge here is to develop a compact WBGT meter with, for example, an air temperature sensor, a humidity sensor and a thermistor in a black globe and integrate it with WBGT Tracker. Most traditional WBGT thermometers on the market are bulky and not that portable like WBGT Tracker.

When on-site measurement is implemented, WBGT Tracker would be able to notify athletes and coaches on the field/court of any sudden rises in WBGT with, for example, alarm sounds and text messages. It can also remind them how often and how long they should take breaks.

Another improvement is to adjust NOAA's forecasts based on where WBGT Tracker is used. Although WBGT forecasts are carefully calculated in NDFD [22], they can be very different from the actual WBGT on particular ground surfaces. For example, in tennis, hard courts are the most common surface type, which is made of concrete and/or asphalt. Both materials absorb heat more and raise air temperature more than natural surfaces [5]. According to recent research findings, WBGT measurements on tennis hard courts are higher than a standard WBGT estimate [23]. The difference/error increases proportionally as the estimated WBGT increases. It is nearly 1°C (1.8°F) when the estimated WBGT is higher than 87.8°F (31°C). Therefore, it might make sense for WBGT Tracker to adjust NOAA's forecast when used for tennis practices or matches on hard courts.

5.6 Conclusion

WBGT Tracker implements a widely-accepted heat safety policy for outdoor athletes [12] and allows them to be aware of the environmental conditions for their activities. This chapter describes how to set up hardware and software components to build WBGT Tracker. Its Python code is available at [21].

References

[1] S. King, Olympics 2024: How extreme weather could impact Paris games, BBC, June 2024.

[2] British Association for Sustainable Sport, Rings of Fire: Heat Risks at the 2024 Paris Olympics, 2024.

[3] D. J. Casa and R. L. Stearns, Preventing Sudden Death in Sport and Physical Activity. 2nd edition, Jones & Bartlett Learning, 2017.

[4] National Federation of State High School Associations, Heat Illness Prevention, online course, https://nfhslearn.com/.

[5] N. Raukar and J. Weaver, Heat Illness Prevention – Keep the Marching Band Playing, National Federation of State High School Associations, 2022.

[6] E. R. Nadel, C. B. Wenger, M. F. Roberts, J. A. Stolwijk, and E. Cafarelli, Physiological defenses against hyperthermia of exercise, Annals of the New York Academy of Sciences, Vol. 1, Issue 1, 1977.

[7] National Institute for Occupational Safety and Health, Heat Stress – Heat Related Illness, 2022.

[8] C. P. Yaglou and D. Minard, Control of Heat Casualties at Military Training Centers, American Medical Association Archives of Industrial Health, 16(4), 302–316, 1957.

[9] United States Tennis Association, 2018 US Open Tennis Championships Extreme Weather Policy, 2018.

[10] United States Soccer Federation, U.S. Soccer Heat Guidelines, http://www.recognizetorecover.org/environmental.

[11] D. J. Casa, J. K. DeMartini, M. F. Bergeron, D. Csillan, E. R. Eichner, R. M. Lopez, M. S. Ferrara, K. C. Miller, F. O'Connor, M. N. Sawka, and S. W. Yeargin, National Athletic Trainers' Association Position Statement: Exertional Heat Illnesses, Journal of Athletic Training, 50(9), 2015.

[12] A. Grundstein, C. Williams, M. Phan, E. Cooper, Regional heat safety thresholds for athletics in the contiguous United States, Applied Geography. Volume 56, 2015.

[13] National Federation of State High School Associations, Heat Acclimatization and Heat Illness Prevention Position Statement, April 2022.

[14] J. Cates and J. D. Rheeling, Wet Bulb Globe Temperature (WBGT) – Why Should Your School Be Using It?, National Federation of State High School Associations, 2023.

[15] https://www.miaa.net/educational-athletics/sports-medicine

[16] Massachusetts Interscholastic Athletic Association, MIAA Heat Modification Policy, August 2021.

[17] https://shop.pimoroni.com/products/inky-phat

[18] https://vlab.noaa.gov/web/mdl/ndfd

[19] https://github.com/pimoroni/inky

[20] https://geocoder.readthedocs.io/

[21] https://github.com/HSSBoston/wbgt

[22] NOAA Meteorological Development Laboratory, MDL Leads the Way in Providing Wet Bulb Globe Temperature Forecasts to the Public, 2021.

[23] H. Yamaguchi, T. Mori, H. Hanano, K. Oishi, K. Ikeue, Y. Yamamoto and K Ishii, Using wet-bulb globe temperature meters to examine the effect of heat on various tennis court surfaces, Scientific Reports, 14, 15548, 2024.

Biography

Hanna Suzuki is a 9th grader who loves reading, music, playing tennis, camping, and hanging out with her friends. She is a founding organizer of two international hackathons: PhysTech and AnimalHack. She has experienced coding with Lego WeDo, Scratch and Squeak Smalltalk since she was a kindergarten student. Most of her recent projects use Python and Raspberry Pi. She is a Python Certified Entry-level Programmer. Hanna won two Global Championships (2022 and 2021) and a Global Finalist Honorable Mention (2023) in the NASA International Space Apps Challenge. She was selected as one of 10 national finalists (2024) and the Massachusetts state merit winner (2023) in the 3M Young Scientist Challenge. Hanna has been active to serve regional, nation-wide, and international K-12 communities by sharing her skills and experience in coding and electronics. Her service was recognized by the President of the United States, and she received Gold Medals of the President's Volunteer Service Award in 2023 and 2024. Hanna also studies piano at the New England Conservatory Preparatory School and has been invited to the Carnegie Hall for her recitals eight times.

Chapter 6

Active+

Vasipalli Eshan Aditya

Global Indian International School
27 Punggol Field Walk
Singapore 828649

vasipallieshan@gmail.com
GitHub profile: eshangonemad

Abstract

Active+ is a unique and intuitive solution to help promote fitness and help end-users achieve their fitness goals by providing widely sought-after features that people usually struggle to find on the internet. The web application makes use of client-side features that enable anyone to use the application, Moreover, it can be run on any device ensuring widespread use by all demographics. The application makes use of the Fitbit API to ensure reliable health data is displayed.

6.1 Introduction

The modern world is plagued with poor health mismanagement and expensive health-tracking applications that cause disdain in anticipating users. This sort of rejection can lead to more health problems in the long run. Moreover, many tools are being pursued on the Internet, and looking for them is a pain. Additionally, the user metrics displayed on health apps are space-consuming and confuse the user.

To solve this tormenting issue, I developed a mobile application to track steps and health data, but realized it is not effective as we receive crude health data. Then, I used the FitBit API to get reliable health telemetry data that can be used within the application. After much research on statistical graphs, I decided to use concentric circles which are much easier and aesthetically pleasing for the users.

6.2 Active+

Our web design mainly consists of two pages, The "You" Page and the Home Page. The user initially begins on the Homepage where all the user metrics are displayed using the concentric circles format. The health metrics that are shown are the "Total Sleep Time", "Total water drunk", "Active Minutes" and "Total Steps". We have a water reminder right underneath the user metrics so that the user can drink water regularly. A quote is displayed to motivate the user into focusing on their health more. A welcome back text is on the top of the page to make users welcome so that they can actively work out. The concentric circles graph has a compact and minimalistic design that showcases all the data in a small area. All of this can be seen on Fig. 1.

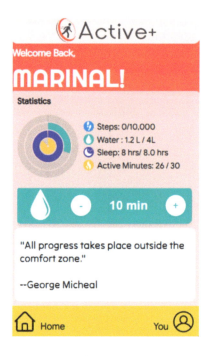

Fig. 1: Active+ "Home Page"

Upon new data from the Fitbit API, the concentric circles along with the text on the side update to show this updated data.

The "You Page" consists of a variety of tools and features that are designed to enhance the user experience, providing hassle free access to all the tools that users usually search for online. The "You Page" provides features such as "BMI calculators," "Mindfulness sessions," "Water Intake Calculator," "Medicine Tracker" and a "To-Do List" to ensure that people stay focused on their fitness goals and do not get distracted by the Internet. These features can be seen on Fig. 2.

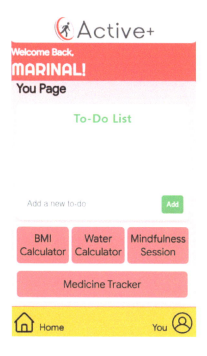

Fig. 2: The "You Page"

The pictures of the tools are shown in Fig. 3.

6.3 Use Cases

Our intuitive health metrics system is suitable for all users and demographics. There is nothing more saddening than seeing your own health deteriorate, after achieving so much in life. Active+ aims to motivate users into improving their lifestyle through the various tools.

Fig. 3: Various parts of the app

This application can be customizable depending on the use case, for example the product can be used for business purposes for tracking employee health, moreover the health metrics can help employers reward and encourage active health in the company.

6.4 Setup

Since this is a client-side web application, it does not require too many dependencies, A Fitbit user token and a Fitbit registered app is required. After the token is placed within the application, the web site can start displaying user data. A web server is required to host it so that users can use the app. More details can be found on the project's GitHub repository on: https://github.com/eshangonemad/Active-

6.5 Future Plans

We plan to improve upon this application to add more features, a few features we are keen on implementing are "Leaderboard Systems," "Community Pages," "Facility Booking," "Healthy Food Recipes" and "Reward Systems."

6.6 Conclusion

Active+ simplifies health tracking by leveraging reliable data from the Fitbit API and presenting it in an intuitive, aesthetically pleasing format. With its dual-page interface, the application offers a seamless user experience, featuring a comprehensive Home Page for health metrics and a versatile "You Page" with additional tools like BMI calculators, mindfulness sessions, and water intake reminders.

Active+ addresses common issues in traditional health apps and is adaptable for various demographics and business use. Future enhancements, including leaderboard systems, community pages, facility booking, healthy food recipes, and reward systems, will further engage and benefit users, solidifying Active+ as an essential tool for a healthier lifestyle.

Biography

Vasipalli Eshan Aditya is a high school student actively pursuing knowledge in the field of computer science. With a keen interest in technology, Eshan has demonstrated remarkable creativity and design skills. He has managed marketing teams for numerous events and has a knack for designing and programming software.

Chapter 7

PushUpPro

Anshul Kotagiri

Rock Hill High School
16061 N Coit Rd
Frisco, TX 75035, USA

Abstract

This project is an innovative fitness application that combines computer vision technology with a user-friendly web interface to create a push-up counter and form analyzer. Built using Streamlit for the front end, the app offers a seamless user experience with easy navigation between sections such as Home, How It Works, and Instructions. The core functionality leverages advanced computer vision techniques, utilizing OpenCV and MediaPipe's pose estimation model to accurately detect and analyze the user's body position during push-ups. The application processes video frames in real time, calculating critical angles of the body (elbow, shoulder, and hip) to determine the correct form and count repetitions. It provides immediate visual feedback on the video feed, displaying the push-up count, form quality, and even specific instructions like "Up," "Down," or "Fix Form." This real-time analysis and feedback system makes it an excellent tool for fitness enthusiasts and beginners, helping them improve their push-up technique and track their progress.

7.1 Inspiration

The inspiration for my workout project, PushUpPro, came from recognizing a significant issue. Millions of Americans suffer from health issues that could be mitigated through regular exercise, yet many choose not to work out. Many factors—such as lack of time, motivation, access to facilities, and knowledge about effective routines—hinder people from engaging in physical activity. This understanding sparked the idea of creating PushUpPro. This web app comprehensively addresses these barriers, particularly the lack of leisure time, transport, childcare facilities, money, and embarrassment about body shape.

7.2 Usage of Mediapipe and OpenCV and Logic of Push-Up Counter

The push-up counter utilizes OpenCV and MediaPipe to provide an accurate and interactive workout-tracking experience. MediaPipe is employed for pose detection, leveraging its pose estimation model to identify key body landmarks. The `poseDetector` class initializes MediaPipe's pose detection with various configurable parameters, enabling the detection of body landmarks such as joints. Once the landmarks are detected, the `findPose` method processes each frame, converting the image from BGR to RGB format, and uses MediaPipe to identify the pose landmarks. These landmarks can be optionally drawn on the image for visual feedback.

The `findPosition` method extracts the coordinates of the detected landmarks and returns them as a list, providing the necessary data to analyze the user's form. Additionally, it can draw circles on the detected landmarks to visually indicate their positions. The `findAngle` method calculates the angles between three specified landmarks: the elbow, shoulder, and hip joints. This angle calculation is crucial for determining the user's form during a push-up, as the angles help identify whether the user is in the "up" or "down" position.

OpenCV is used for video capture and frame processing. It captures video frames from the webcam and processes each frame to detect the pose, calculate the necessary angles, and count push-ups based on the user's movements. The angle of the elbow, shoulder, and hip joints are particularly important for determining the user's form. Specific angle ranges correspond to a push-up's "up" and "down" positions. The code includes checks to ensure the user's form is correct, such as verifying that the elbow is at a specific angle when the user is in the "down" position and that the hip is in a particular position.

The logic for counting push-ups involves interpolating the elbow angle to a percentage, which helps determine the push-up phase (0% for "down" and 100% for "up"). The state (up or down) is managed using a direction flag. When the user reaches the "down" position, the direction changes, and when the user reaches the "up" position, the count is incremented if the form is correct. Visual feedback is provided on the frame, showing the percentage, count, and remarks about the user's form. This combination of MediaPipe's pose detection and OpenCV's video processing capabilities allows the application to accurately count push-ups and provide real-time feedback on the user's form, enhancing the workout experience.

Fig 1: Home Page

Final push-up count and form analysis. The image shows the completion of a workout session with the total number of push-ups completed and the percentage of the current push-up phase.

7.3 Usage of Streamlit as Front End

7.3.1 Home Page

Fig 2: Home Page

Home Page of the PushUpPro application. This page serves as the landing page where users can start the push-up counter by clicking the button.

7.3.2 Instructional Pages

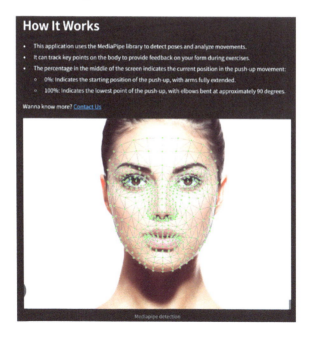

Fig 3: Instructional Pages

The "How It Works" page explains the technical details and how the push-up counter works, while the "Instructions" page provides guidelines on how to perform push-ups correctly using the app.

7.3.3 Homepage Frontend Code

The following code snippet shows the implementation of the homepage (Section 7.3.1), including the navigation and button functionalities for different sections.

```python
import streamlit as st
from home import show_home
from how_it_works import show_how_it_works
from instructions import show_instructions

def main():
    st.sidebar.title("Navigation")
    home_button = st.sidebar.button("Home")
    how_it_works_button = st.sidebar.button("How It Works")
    instructions_button = st.sidebar.button("Instructions")

    if home_button:
        show_home()
    elif how_it_works_button:
        show_how_it_works()
    elif instructions_button:
        show_instructions()
    else:
        show_home()

if __name__ == "__main__":
    main()
```

7.3.4 Instructional Pages Code

The following code snippet illustrates the implementation of the "How It Works" page (Section 7.3.2), detailing the structure and information presented on the page.

```python
import streamlit as st

def show_how_it_works():
    st.markdown("""
    ## How It Works
    - This application uses the MediaPipe library to detect poses and
analyze movements.
    - It can track key points on the body to provide feedback on your
form during exercises.
    - The percentage in the middle of the screen indicates the current
position in the push-up movement:
```

```
        - 0%: Indicates the starting position of the push-up, with arms
fully extended.
        - 100%: Indicates the lowest point of the push-up, with elbows
bent at approximately 90 degrees.
        """)

    st.markdown("Wanna know more? [Contact Us]" +\
            "(mailto:kotagirianshul@gmail.com)")
    st.image("mediapipe.png",
            caption="Mediapipe detection",
            use_column_width=True)
```

The following code snippet illustrates the implementation of the "Instructions" page (Section 7.3.2), detailing the structure and information presented on the pages.

```
import streamlit as st

def show_instructions():
    st.markdown("""
    ## Instructions
    - Follow the bar on the top. Use it to understand when to go down
and when to go up during push-ups.
    - To make sure the program works effectively, please make sure you
are in push-up position and the camera is an appropriate distance away.
    - You will be given 30 seconds to complete as many push-ups as you
can, and based on your results, the program will provide an AI-gener-
ated plan of action that will help you further your workout goals.
    """)

    st.markdown("Having trouble? [Contact Us]" +\
            "(mailto:kotagirianshul@gmail.com)")
    st.image("final.png",
            caption="Finished workout",
            use_column_width=True)
```

7.4 Future Steps

The next significant step for the project is to incorporate body type detection to create personalized plans for users to increase their push-up count each week. This will require gathering information about the user's body type and specific form using Mediapipe. The data can then be fed into a specialized AI model, which will provide feedback on how users can improve their diet and form to enhance their weekly push-up performance.

Additionally, an improvement to the user experience would be to deliver feedback through audio instead of visual prompts. This way, users won't need to constantly look at the screen for feedback from the application.

7.5 Conclusion

Overall, PushUpPro is a powerful tool designed to address common barriers to physical exercise by providing an easy-to-use, interactive push-up counter and form analyzer. By leveraging advanced computer vision technologies, it offers real-time feedback and guidance to users, helping them improve their push-up technique and overall fitness. The seamless user interface, built using Streamlit, ensures a smooth and intuitive user experience, allowing easy navigation between sections.

Participating and presenting in PhysTech 2024 was an enriching experience. Throughout the project, several significant challenges require careful thought, decision-making, and troubleshooting through trial and error. One major obstacle is learning and utilizing Streamlit for the front end, ensuring a user-friendly interface. Additionally, integrating OpenCV and MediaPipe into the program would present considerable difficulties.

For the complete code, refer to the Project GitHub repository: `https://github.com/PassionateCodingMan/PushUpPro2`.

Biography

Anshul Kotagiri is a passionate developer in his senior year of high school. With a keen interest in technology and its potential to drive innovation, Anshul aspires to pursue a degree in Management Information Systems. He has demonstrated a solid commitment to leveraging technology to solve real-world problems throughout his academic journey. Anshul has gained hands-on experience by working on various technical and business. His enthusiasm for technology extends beyond the classroom; he participates in competitions, has a tech internship, and conducts AI research. His drive and technical skills position him as a future leader in Management Information Systems Field, where he aims to make a meaningful impact through innovative solutions.

Chapter 8

Soccer Display

Hiroki Kudara

Dedham High School
Dedham, MA 02026, USA

Abstract

This project involves the utilization of raspberry pi and an e-paper display in order to create a display that is able to show certain data that revolve around a singular soccer player of your choice. This project relies heavily on API databases such as native-stats.org, which is the cornerstone for this project. This requires you to create your own account with a unique api token. If done correctly, this allows you to see data on a specific player.

8.1 Introduction

Professional soccer matches are played at various times across the week. These factors cause problems when trying to watch every single soccer match your favorite soccer player participates in.

This project features a raspberry pi powered display, which is capable of displaying stats for a specific soccer player and the team they play for, such as but not limited to: the final score, which team they played against, and the date of the match. This information is acquired from an API from native-stats.org, as mentioned before. This project then finds all of this information for the latest 3 games your player-of-choice scored in. After the information has been gathered, the code then proceeds to use the e-paper display module to display this information on the (2.13" x 1") display. Fig. 1 shows an example of the completed project.

Fig. 1: The actual information shown on the e-paper display.

8.2 Use Cases

This project was built to help people figure out the outcome of the matches they have missed, especially for people who have other extracurriculars or plans during the matches, which causes them to miss the matches due to the overlap in their schedules. For example, if you wanted to watch a game that involved your favorite soccer player, but the scheduled time for the soccer game overlapped perfectly with your badminton lesson, you would have to miss the game, and watch the highlights of the match just to see if your favorite player had scored or not. However, with this project, you are able to see if your favorite soccer player had scored in that game in a matter of seconds after running the code and looking at the information that is shown on the e-paper display.

8.3 Hardware Setup

In order to create your own soccer display you will need the following components:

- Raspberry Pi 3 Model A+ & MicroSD card (1x)
- Raspberry Pi Power Supply
- E-paper Display (2.13" x 1")

First, make sure you have the e-paper display. (Fig. 2). The e-paper has a display and a plastic part below it that accepts 40 pins. Then, gently connect the 40-pin connector on the back of the display to the Raspberry Pi 3 Model A+ and MicroSD card. (Fig. 3).

Fig. 2: E-paper Display

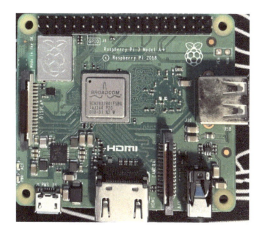

Fig. 3: Raspberry Pi 3 Model A+

Fig. 4: Raspberry Pi and the E-paper display

You will then take the power supply adapter and plug it in the Raspberry Pi. If done correctly, your hardware should look like Fig. 4.

After all of this, the hardware is set up and ready to go.

8.4 Coding

```
import argparse, qrcode, inky_paste, subprocess
from footballdata import getFootballData
from pprint import pprint
from PIL import Image, ImageFont, ImageDraw
from font_hanken_grotesk import HankenGroteskBold
from font_hanken_grotesk import HankenGroteskMedium
from font_intuitive import Intuitive
from inky.auto import auto

# Heung-min Son's player ID: 170281
apiToken = ""
url = "https://api.football-data.org/v4/" +\
      "persons/170281/matches?e=GOAL"

try:
    responseDict = getFootballData(url, apiToken)
    pprint(responseDict)
    matches = responseDict["matches"][:3]
    pprint(matches)
except Exception as e:
    print(f"Error fetching football data: {e}")
    exit(1)

try:
    inky_display = auto(ask_user=True, verbose=True)
except TypeError:
    raise TypeError("Update the Inky library to >= v1.1.0")

try:
    inky_display.set_border(inky_display.WHITE)
except NotImplementedError:
    pass

scale_size = 1.0
padding = 0

if inky_display.resolution == (400, 300):
    scale_size = 2.20
    padding = 15
elif inky_display.resolution == (600, 448):
    scale_size = 2.20
    padding = 30
elif inky_display.resolution == (250, 122):
    scale_size = 1.30
    padding = -5

img = Image.new("P", inky_display.resolution)
draw = ImageDraw.Draw(img)

font_path = "/usr/share/fonts/truetype/dejavu/DejaVuSans-Bold.ttf"
```

```
font_large = ImageFont.truetype(font_path, 24)
font_medium = ImageFont.truetype(font_path, 18)
font_small = ImageFont.truetype(font_path, 12)

y_top = int(inky_display.height * (5.0 / 10.0))
for y in range(y_top, inky_display.height):
    for x in range(0, inky_display.width):
        img.putpixel((x, y), inky_display.WHITE)

def add_match_details(draw, match, y_offset):
    utcDate = match["utcDate"]
    date = utcDate.split("T")[0]
    yr, mo, day = date.split("-")
    print(yr, mo, day)

    matchId = str(match["id"])
    print(matchId)
    print(match["homeTeam"]["name"], "v.s.",
        match["awayTeam"]["name"])
    print(match["homeTeam"]["shortName"], "v.s.",
        match["awayTeam"]["shortName"])
    print(match["homeTeam"]["tla"], "v.s.",
        match["awayTeam"]["tla"])
    print(match["score"]["fullTime"]["home"], "-",
        match["score"]["fullTime"]["away"])

    webpage = "https://native-stats.org/match/" + matchId
    print("For more details, see: " + webpage)

    date_text = f"{yr}-{mo}-{day}"
    score_text = f"{match['score']['fullTime']['home']} -
{match['score']['fullTime']['away']}"
    teams_text = f"{match['homeTeam']['tla']} v.s.
{match['awayTeam']['tla']}"

    draw.text((0, y_offset), date_text,
            inky_display.RED, font=font_large)
    draw.text((0, y_offset + 15), teams_text,
            inky_display.BLACK, font=font_medium)
    draw.text((0, y_offset + 27), score_text,
            inky_display.BLACK, font=font_medium)

y_offset = 0
for match in matches:
    add_match_details(draw, match, y_offset)
    y_offset += 40

inky_display.set_image(img)
inky_display.show()
```

The 13th line of code is essential for this project as this code will not function without an API token from native-stats.org. If you would like to use this code for yourself, please register an account and create a free API token and paste it in between the quotation marks.

8.5 Future Steps

This project is currently able to display statistics regarding soccer matches played by a specific player. However, this data is only shown on the display, and moving forward, I will be adding Kintone support for easy data access from other devices, such as a mobile device. This requires me to create a Kintone app, and I am planning to add a QR code to the display which would redirect you to the app where you will be able to see all the data.

8.6 Conclusion

In conclusion, this project demonstrates the utilization of a Raspberry Pi and an e-paper display in order to create a functional and informative tool for soccer enthusiasts. By taking advantage of API databases such as native-stats.org, enthusiasts can access and display up-to-date statistics for their favorite soccer players, making it easier to keep track of performances even when they cannot watch the matches live. This project not only offers a practical solution to the problem of missing games but also provides a foundation for further improvements, such as incorporating Kintone support for more data accessibility. Future developments, including the addition of QR codes, will further enhance the user experience and expand the utility of this project.

Biography

Hiroki Kudara is a 10th grader who loves video games, chess, soccer, kendo and hanging out with friends. He has been playing soccer since he was 9 years old. He also practices Kendo, which is a Japanese martial art that originated from traditional swordsmanship, specifically kenjutsu. Practitioners use bamboo swords called "Shinai" and protective gear to practice Kendo. Hiroki is a co-founder of PhysTech. His project won the Honorable Mention Award in PhysTech 2024.

About the Editors

Shun Nagata is a sports enthusiast who loves data analytics and coding. He co-founded PhysTech and co-chaired its inaugural edition in 2024. Currently a 11th grader, Shun is a starting center-midfielder in the varsity soccer team while playing on a club team. He has won a few league/tournament championships, such as a championship in the local high school league of eight schools. He is also a JV baseball player. Shun has a strong interest in data analytics, especially sabermetrics. He studies various baseball stats and practices them in fantasy baseball leagues. He even developed a new stat category of his own and has been analyzing it with real game datasets. Shun exercises his Python coding skill to implement the baseball stats and build Internet of Things devices. He has earned the Certified Entry-Level Python Programmer (PCEP) certificate. Shun has been volunteering in many ways for various communities, such as teaching others about the Internet of Things devices. His service was awarded by the president of the U.S., and he received a Gold Medal of the President's Volunteer Service Award. He won the Silver Prize at AnimalHack 2023.

Sarasa Ouchi is a first-year college student majoring computer science. She co-founded PhysTech and co-chaired its inaugural edition in 2024. She also served as a founding chair of AnimalHack 2023 (https://animalhack.org/) and published its proceedings as the corresponding editor. She formed and led a team of five high school and middle school students and won a Global Finalist Honorable Mention at the 2023 NASA International Space Apps Challenge. Her project was featured by a newspaper in the New York area. She regularly teaches Python coding to K-12 students while continuing to hone her skills by organizing and participating in hackathons. Sarasa's commitment to community service has been recognized with a United Nations National Service Award. Her fascination with the versatility of programming fuels her continuous learning journey, culminating in her attainment of an associate-level programming certification from the Python Institute. Driven by curiosity and a desire to explore the endless possibilities of programming, Sarasa strives to push boundaries and inspire others in this field.

www.ingramcontent.com/pod-product-compliance
Lightning Source LLC
Chambersburg PA
CBHW041143050326
40689CB00001B/462